A588

P9-CJV-048

Sometimes
I Wonder About Me

SOMETIMES I WONDER ABOUT ME

Teenagers and Mental Health

Marion Howard

Continuum · New York

1984

The Continuum Publishing Company
370 Lexington Avenue
New York, New York 10017

Printed in the United States of America

Library of Congress Cataloging in Publication Data

Howard, Marion, 1936–
Sometimes I wonder about me.

1. Adolescent psychopathology. 2. Adolescent
psychology. 3. Mental health services. I. Title.
RJ503.H67 1983   155.5   83-7351
ISBN 0-8264-0199-6

To my mother
whose caring and support
helped all her family

Contents

Preface

Adolescence is an important formative time. During adolescence young people move away from childhood toward adulthood. This changing process is often a stressful one for adolescents and their parents. Sometimes attitudes, feelings, or events get in the way of the young person's being able to use the adolescent period to best advantage. More seriously, problems in living can actually interrupt the adolescent's developmental process. Young people and adults alike may have difficulty distinguishing between normal adolescent adjustment problems and problems of a more serious nature requiring intervention.

Sometimes I Wonder About Me, therefore, is written to help both young people and adults understand that a wide range of feelings, attitudes and behaviors can occur during adolescence that are part of what is thought of as normal. However, problems in living that are continuous, unusually severe, or destructive to the adolescent may be of a serious nature and should at least be evaluated by a mental-health professional to see if intervention is warranted.

The stories of *Sometimes I Wonder About Me* are intended to encourage young people to overcome possible negative images of mental-health services, and to seek help if and when they feel they need it. Age-appropriate mental-health services can help remove obstacles to growth and free adolescents from attitudes and behaviors that will limit their lives and undermine future freedom and independence. The book is also intended to give adults support for seeking mental-health services for adolescents who seem excessively troubled. The purpose of the commentary that runs throughout the stories is to clarify issues and add information of interest to teenagers, their parents, and other concerned adults.

I wish to thank Suzanne P. Ellington for the time she spent in reading drafts and offering suggestions. A special thank you must go to my family for their patience and support during the writing of this book, particularly to my daughter and son.

1

I'm Me and This Is Where I Am

MARTIN

Martin shifted gears and glanced down at the gas gauge on his family's old car. It was registering nearly empty. Martin smiled in satisfaction. Now he would be able to find out what he had always wanted to know—exactly how far down the needle would go before the car ran out of gas. He knew the car didn't stop when the needle first touched the red zone. He'd even driven the car a couple of times when the needle had been almost halfway down into the red. But what he didn't know was, whether you ran out of gas when it was in the middle of the red, at the end of the red, or out of the red.

Martin's mom and dad didn't have much money so whenever Martin got to use the car, which wasn't often, it rarely had even a quarter of a tank of gas in it. And since Martin had little or no money for gas, it was very important to know how far he could go on what little was in there.

Martin turned the corner. This driving around going nowhere was kind of boring. He turned another corner.

"Martin! Martin!" A chorus of voices called his name. He slowed the car and looked around. All six cheerleaders from his school were chasing him. He stopped the car wondering what was going on.

Jennie was the first to reach the car. She had a pleading look on her face.

"Martin, please. Can you help us out? There's combined cheerleading practice for all the high schools over at Briarcliff High. The school bus was supposed to come back and take us after they dropped off all the kids, but it hasn't shown up. We could take the public bus but that would make us about a half hour late and the practice only lasts an hour and a half. Please, Martin, could you take us? Please?"

Martin looked at Jennie's face. To him she was the prettiest cheerleader of them all. Martin didn't date anyone, let alone a cheerleader, but if he could fantasize about whom he would like to date, it would be Jennie. Fat chance, though. He was surprised she even knew his name.

"Sure, I'd be happy to," he answered.

"Ooooh," the girls screamed their appreciation and piled into the car. Jennie opened the front door and slid in next to him. She pressed close to him to make room for Tina in the front seat. The other four girls sat in the back.

"Ohh, Martin," Jennie cooed as they started off. "You will just never know how grateful I am to you. This means a lot to us. We've been looking forward to this joint practice for a long time. You see . . ."

Martin didn't care about cheerleaders' practice and who did what with whom, but he had never before had the sensation of his car being filled with chattering girls. It was kinda fun. He glanced around to see if anyone else from school was watching, but no one was. Too bad. Anyway, the best part was having Jennie sit next to him and talk in his ear about the stupid cheerleading.

Martin cut down Walden Street and over LaVista. Going through the residential section was faster than going down any of the main streets. He turned right on Twin Oaks Drive.

"Oh, look at those gorgeous mum plants," one girl cried. "Oh, fall is such a wonderful time. I just love it."

Martin already knew from his cousin Patti that girls just "loved" everything. Patti just loved jeans, just loved Olivia Newton-John, just loved Springer Spaniel puppies, just loved mint ice cream with chocolate chips (truth to tell Martin kinda liked that too).

Martin turned left on Ridgecliff. Then it happened. The motor went cough, cough sputter, sputter, and died. The car rolled gently over to the side of the street and came to a stop.

"So that's where it is," Martin cried in satisfaction. "I was sure it was going to be when it got off the red but instead it's just before the end of the red."

The girls were moaning in the back, "Oh, what's happened?"

"Martin, what are you talking about?" Jennie asked.

"The gas gauge," Martin put his finger on the glass in front of the needle. "You see it ran out of gas right here and I thought it would be over here."

"Out of gas!" A wailing chorus arose from the back seat.

"Martin, you mean we're out of gas?" Jennie cried.

"Yes," said Martin in a pleased tone.

"And you knew we were going to run out of gas?" Jennie asked incredulously.

"Well, I didn't know when," Martin said. Again he patiently repeated, "You see I thought it would be over here, but it's right here."

"You planned this?" Tina's voice also sounded incredulous.

"Well, I didn't plan it to be while you were along," Martin replied, turning to look at her, "But I did plan to run out of gas. You see I got curious about exactly how far I could go before the car would actually run out of gas. Then whenever I drove I would know for sure when I had to stop to get . . ."

Martin did not get a chance to finish. The car doors opened and angry girls began piling out all sides. "Of all the rotten things to do . . ." "The stupidest . . ." "Way out here . . ." "We're not even on a busline." "We'll never get . . ."

Martin was amazed at how angry the girls were.

"Look," he said, "I didn't know it was going to happen here . . ."

As Jennie got out, she turned around and put her face back into the car. "Some knight in shining armor you turned out to be. You're a clown in an old tin can." Then she backed up and slammed the door. Martin watched her run to catch up with the other girls. They were already half way up the drive of the nearest house looking for a telephone to use.

Martin was sorry he had made Jennie mad. But he hadn't planned to have it happen when she was along. He hadn't even planned to have her along at all. It was the girls who asked him for a ride. He didn't ask them.

Martin sat behind the wheel a while longer. Then he shrugged and glanced back down at the gas gauge. So that's where it was. He really had thought it was going to be when it got to the end of the red.

Well, he'd best go get some gas. The girls hadn't come back out of the house yet. Martin didn't want to see them again today. Besides, it was going to be a long walk to a gas station from where he was. Before he'd picked up the girls, he had been cruising in an area that had a couple of gas stations, but he was way out where there was none now.

Martin got out of the car, shut the door, and started walking back in the direction he had come. He half smiled, half grimaced. Well, it wasn't a bad day for a walk. There would be those "gorgeous mums," and after all he just "loved" fall.

LYDIA

Lydia sat on her bed. It should have been comforting being back in her room, but it wasn't. It seemed strange being here even though she had been gone only four days.

I should want to be here, she thought. At least that's what I told the policeman when he asked me if I wanted to go home. But now that I'm here, I'm not sure. Her terrible sense of despair had not been changed by the few days of wandering. The hurt, she learned, was with her regardless of where she was.

Lydia heard the phone ring downstairs. Then her mother's voice said, "Yes, she's back . . . Yes, thank God, she's safe." Then, "No, I still don't know why she ran away. We haven't had a chance to talk . . . Of course, I'll call you soon . . . And thank you for calling." The receiver clinked against the holder.

"Lydia," her mother called up the stairs, "I'm fixing you some dinner. Why don't you take a bath and get into some fresh clothes. You'll feel better."

Lydia's spirits sagged further. Count on her mother to not understand. It wasn't "Lydia—the heck with dinner—what's troubling you? How can I help?" It was just life as usual and, of course, an order—"Do this so this will happen."

Lydia lay back on her bed. But then even if her mother had asked her, "What's troubling you, Lydia?" Lydia probably would not have answered. Her mother wouldn't understand. She never did. Somehow even when Lydia most wanted to be close to her mother and tried, something kept them apart. Lydia couldn't tell what it was. It just never worked for them somehow. It never had. Or if it had, it was long before her father left and her mother remarried.

Lydia felt isolated from her family. Her real father had been a puzzle to her even though she and her brother, Finney, adored him. He could be totally charming sometimes and, at other times, very rejecting, even cruel. People said Lydia was more like her father and Finney more like her mother. Nevertheless, because Finney was a boy, Lydia felt her father liked him better. Lydia was always trying to prove herself to her father.

Lydia's father drank. A couple of times he hit Lydia, even once knocking her across the room. Although she knew it was because he had had too much to drink, secretly she felt it was also part of her never quite being what he wanted her to be.

——————————

One way to stay mentally healthy is to know oneself— one's strengths, one's weaknesses, one's values and goals. Adolescence is a time when young people take time to find out about themselves. In the process of growing towards adulthood, young people must adjust to bodily changes, develop an identity as a man or a woman, establish a personal set of values, gain more independence from adult control, and decide how they will support themselves in the future. Emotionally healthy people do not tell themselves they are stupid or unattractive or bumbling. However, they also don't believe they are smarter than anyone else in the world, or handsomer or more capable than anyone else. Emotionally healthy people are realistic about who they are, what their potential is. They utilize their strengths and attempt to overcome their weaknesses. They are aware the world around them is not perfect, but that doesn't reduce their trying to develop their lives to the fullest.

——————————

Lydia sighed. She supposed Jim, her new stepfather, would be home with Finney and her half-sister, Marcia. It was ironic. Just like her real dad, she felt her new father liked Finney better too. He had already had a daughter in Marcia, so a son was a novelty. Lydia was just an extra daughter. Finney already called him "Dad." Lydia could never bring herself to do that.

"Oh, father, where are you?" Lydia murmured. Lydia still blamed her mother for the quarreling that went on between Lydia's mother and her real father. Lydia remembered she used to dream that one day her father would come to her and say, "Let's you and I get out of this place together; just leave Finney and your mom." But that didn't happen; instead, one day her father and mother both announced they were getting a divorce. They said they had agreed that Lydia and Finney would live with their mother and that their father would visit them occasionally. Lydia was dumbfounded and depressed. She desperately needed someone to talk to, to help her make sense out of what was going on, to help her adjust. But there was no one.

Then came the endless waits for her father's visits. It was even more painful when people commented that Finney was so much like his mother. It emphasized that the parent she was like, her father, was now missing. And there were all the broken promises. Her father would say he would come and take them to the zoo or something. Sometimes he would arrive two hours late with a change in what they were going to do; sometimes he just wouldn't show at all.

Often when he didn't come, Lydia would blame herself. If only she were prettier or more charming or cleverer, perhaps her father would want to be with her more. She spent hours thinking up things she would do the next time he came, to make him like her more. Then there were other times when her father came unexpectedly and took her and Finney off somewhere to have a wonderful time.

Her mother hated it when her father came unexpectedly and said she thought it was disruptive and inconsiderate for her father to just show up and expect them to drop their plans for him. Lydia thought that attitude was very selfish on the part of her mother, and she resented her mother all the more for not making their father feel welcome whenever he came.

Then two years ago, it had happened. Her father had been killed in a car crash. There were whispers that he had had too much to drink. But it was on a wintry night. Lydia believed it was just that the roads were too icy. There had been a woman with her father who was injured but not killed. Lydia blamed the woman for making her dad be out on a bad night.

Lydia didn't cry very much when her dad died—at least not publicly. She mostly felt angry and cheated. Her dad was the one she was most like. Now she was like no one. She was alone. Her mother's efforts to comfort her just made Lydia all the more angry. Finally she blurted out, "Why couldn't you have been the one to die? Don't you understand, I need him, not you!" Her mother didn't say anything. Lydia knew she must feel very hurt but she didn't care. All she cared about was her father.

In the months following her father's death, Lydia spent more and more time in her room. She let Finney go off and do things with their mother without wanting to go along. Not that there were that many times, since her mother had a busy career to manage besides the two children. But Lydia always excused herself by saying she had too much homework or was too tired when her mother urged her to go somewhere with them. Let them be together. What did she care. Now that her father was gone, Lydia was alone and she might as well stay that way.

Then Lydia met Wayne. It wasn't a spectacular meeting. They had been in the same class for a long time. But somehow they started noticing one another. And then they started dating.

Lydia was never quite sure how it all came about but it changed her entire life. Wayne was a popular boy. He was good in a lot of things and nearly everyone liked him. He was always included in the fun things that went on. Lydia had never been popular, but by going with Wayne she was immediately accepted by all the kids who really mattered.

Wayne made Lydia feel special. She had to catch her breath every once in a while just to assure herself their relationship was real. She wanted to please Wayne as much as she had wanted to please her dad. Unlike her dad, however, Wayne really liked her and seemed to want to please her too.

Lydia suddenly was aware tears were flowing down her face. She had thought the tears were all gone, that there were none left. Yet they were there. But what did it really matter? Her whole life was shattered. It would never be the same again. There was nowhere to go, nothing to do.

Lydia heard her mother coming out of the kitchen. Lydia didn't want to see her mother right yet. She didn't want to see anyone. She didn't want to be anyone.

Lydia remembered the bath she was supposed to be taking. The running water would drown out her crying and the bathroom would give her a place to hide. Slowly she got up off the bed and pulled open the drawer of her dresser. She took out a nightgown and went into the bathroom and turned on the water. She cried for a long while. Then it didn't seem to matter any more whether she cried or not. She slowly got out of her clothes and stepped into the water. She remembered a time when she enjoyed the feel of a warm bath but now she couldn't seem to react to anything. She just felt numb.

Eventually she heard her mother at the bathroom door. "I've got some supper ready. Why don't you get out of the tub now so we can have a quiet dinner together before the rest of the family gets home? I want to talk with you."

Another order—"Do this so this will happen."

Lydia compliantly got out of the tub. She dried herself, put on her nightgown and then went back to her room to get a robe. Her mother stood waiting for her at the top of the stairs.

"I'm not really very hungry," Lydia said.

"Well, a little something will do you good," her mother replied, still standing patiently at the top of the stairs. She came forward and put an arm around Lydia as Lydia came out of her room. They walked downstairs together.

Lydia felt the irony of the motherly affection all of a sudden. Lydia's mother's career had always kept her very busy. Since her mother's remarriage, Lydia had felt her mother had even less time for her. Certainly there hadn't been a time when her mother waited for her at the stairs and put an arm around her on the way to dinner. It had been more like: "Lydia, stop picking on Marcia—she's younger than you."

Lydia sat down at the table. She saw her mother had made her favorite meal—tacos. She took her fork and began picking at her food.

"Dear, I'm so glad to have you back," her mother said as she sat down across the table from her. "You had us all so terribly worried. We're your family and we love you. I don't know what made you think you could solve whatever it is that's bothering you by running away from home. We want you here." Her mother paused.

Lydia kept her eyes down. She nervously picked at some more food.

"Now tell me, what's troubling you dear? Is it something going on at home here? You know Jim loves you just as much as I do."

Lydia shook her head.

"Well, is it something at school then? I know school's never been easy for you, dear, but you always get passing grades. Has something gone wrong at school, dear?"

Lydia shook her head again, wondering how long she would have to endure the questioning.

"Well, if it's breaking up with that young man last week, I told you when it happened that you'd get over it. Things like that happen all the time to young people. You're probably going to go with and break up with many young men before you find the right one."

The pain welled up inside Lydia at her mother's mention of Wayne. She felt she would break down right then in front of her mother. Fortunately the phone rang.

"Excuse me, dear, I'm so sorry to interrupt but with the family gone, I guess I'll just have to get it."

In the background she heard her mother say, "Milly, yes, we've found her . . . No, she's home already . . . Oh, I am too. It's a miracle . . . Why, thank you, dear."

So it was her Aunt Milly. Everyone in the whole world must know she ran away.

Her mother was saying, "Oh, Milly what ever would make you think that? . . . A psychiatrist? . . . No. Lydia is perfectly all right. She's just upset about something . . . No, I don't know what. You know how children are. Plus, it's really not as easy growing up these days. Lydia just needs some time . . . Yes, I know she's been up and down since he died . . . Well, that is another idea. But she's already missed a week of school and . . . I know, Milly, but I'm not sure Jim . . ."

So many symptoms of adolescents who have mental or emotional problems fit in one way or another with those attitudes and behaviors of normal adolescents, that it is difficult at times to know who should be referred to a mental-health professional. Probably the severity, the consistency, and the debilitative nature of the symptoms are the best indicators that an adolescent needs at least an evaluation for problems of a serious nature.

Lydia could sense some aggravation creeping into her mother's voice. She wondered what her aunt was saying.

"Yes, I'll think it over, Milly . . . Of course, dear . . . Yes, that is a possibility . . . Look, Milly, let's talk again next week.

Lydia has just gotten home and I don't think we can make any decisions right now . . . Yes, I know she'd need a passport. Oh I see . . . Well, I'll talk to you next week."

A passport? Lydia wondered what they were talking about. Lydia heard her mother hang up the phone and start back toward the dining room. What if her mother started talking about Wayne again? Lydia felt her stomach churn.

Then Lydia heard the front door opening and a cheery "Hi, ho. Anybody home?" It was Jim's voice. Lydia abruptly stood up. Gathering her robe up above her ankles, she fled upstairs to her room. She closed the door quickly, took off her robe, and got into bed.

She heard the rest of the family entering the dining room and then Jim's voice saying to her mom, "No, my feelings aren't hurt. That's okay. I'll talk to her tomorrow. She's probably tired."

Then Lydia heard whispers and her mother's voice saying, "No, children, not now. You'll see her in the morning." Then in a louder voice, "Finney, I said NOT NOW!"

Lydia was grateful to her mother. Most of the time she and her mother were at each other's throats, but tonight, just for a minute, her mother seemed to understand something anyway.

GEORGE

George threw his books down angrily on his bed and stood staring at them. What the hell did people expect anyway? His dad was on him, his mom was on him, the teachers were on him, his girlfriend was on him, and now even the coach was on him. What the hell did he care? No matter how hard he tried, everyone wanted more.

George flopped down on the bed, pushing his books over the edge as he did. His stomach was in knots. What was wrong with him anyway? George knew he should have gone to the extra basketball practice session. But he hadn't spent any time with Marilyn all week. And when she pleaded with him to skip practice so they could be alone at her house and play records, well, he had just said "shove it" to the basketball practice.

Marilyn was a very popular girl and George really liked her. He figured he had to give her enough attention or she'd find someone else. Girls like Marilyn just didn't sit home. As it was, she complained about how little time he spent with her. Marilyn also told him how she hated going to the basketball games with "the girls." She wanted to sit with a date like "everyone else." Maybe if he'd been the star of the team she would have felt differently, but he wasn't the star. He was a regular player but by no means a star. George tried to think up things to do for Marilyn to make it up to her for not sitting with her, but somehow felt he never succeeded. Often their relationship seemed just a snap away from falling apart.

George couldn't lie still. He rolled over. God, what did they all expect? The coach had yelled at him. The science teacher had bugged him again about getting his mid-semester project in. And his dad, well his dad had threatened him with some sort of stupid punishment if he didn't borrow the Johnsons' lawn mower (theirs was broken) and cut the grass, *today*. Why did the stupid grass have to start growing so early in the spring? Why couldn't it wait till summer when he was out of school?

Damn. George stared up at the ceiling. Why hadn't he borrowed the lawn mower and cut the grass last Saturday when his dad had told him to? Why? Because last Saturday was the first time all week he had had a day to breathe. He'd gone over to Brodie's house in the morning just to say "hi" and check on the used carburetor Brodie was trying to put in that junk heap he called a car. George hadn't expected to stay but he'd gotten involved in trying to figure out whether or not the carburetor was the right one for the car. Then they had gone to the video arcade to play "Wonder Warrior."

It was really disgusting. Some dumb mother was there with three little kids. The line to play "Wonder Warrior" was always long. "Wonder Warrior" was about ten times more popular than Pac-Man had been when it first came out a number of years before. The video store manager said they couldn't make the "Wonder Warrior" machines fast enough— everyone in the country wanted them. That was why his place only had one. Anyway this dumb mother kept feeding in tokens for these three little kids and the little kids didn't know what the heck they were doing and it took forever.

Then George still had to wait for all the kids who did know how to play. When he got the machine finally, he was plain mad. Even though he loved "Wonder Warrior," there was all that pressure from the kids behind him to finish his game while he was still angry from having to wait so long for his turn.

George remembered exactly how he had played "Wonder Warrior." George knew he was supposed to keep changing how Wonder Warrior would kill the enemy—you got more points that way. But he had Wonder Warrior lop off heads mostly. He loved the little computerized expressions when their heads fell off. Take that coach! Take that dad! Take that science teacher! It was only when the amazon women came out to challenge Wonder Warrior that George varied his killing technique. He just couldn't bear to lop off Marilyn's beautiful head. Instead he killed the women in less dramatic ways.

George smiled as he recalled how many amazon women he'd been able to kill before Wonder Warrior got his. Then he frowned. Damn! He knew enough to watch for *the net throw*. Why the hell hadn't he remembered it was going to be coming.

Anyway, by the time George had come back home, it was

well past noon on Saturday and Mr. Johnson wasn't at home. So the grass just sat, his dad just sat and looked at it, and everyone was unhappy.

Now here it was Friday and George must get the lawn mower and cut the grass. His dad had said if Saturday rolled around again and the grass was still uncut, George would have to stay home next week except for school and basketball.

But George didn't move. He just lay on his bed. Finally he rolled over to where he could reach the stereo and turned on some music. It was tuned to BXZ, the rock station in town. The music blared out.

He was still on his bed when his mother got home from work an hour later.

"My goodness, I certainly knew you were home," she said in that overly sweet tone she used when she was annoyed. "I heard that music before I even got in the drive."

"Well," George snapped. "If you didn't want the music, you shouldn't have bought me the damn hi-fi." George was in no mood to hear any more lectures.

"Don't be so touchy," his mother said, a little put off by his strong reply. "I just mentioned I thought it was a little loud."

"Well, I'll shut the damn thing off then." He reached up and switched off the radio.

"I didn't say you had to turn it *off*," his mother quickly rejoined. "I just said *down*." Irritation was building in her voice.

George bounced off the bed, brushed past his mother, and went down the hall to the bathroom. Momentarily he'd be safe in there. Besides, he really had to go. He'd been too riled to bother when he came home.

"George, what do you want for dinner? I've got some of that casserole we had Sunday, or chipped beef for the chipped beef and biscuit thing I make." His mother was standing outside the bathroom door.

God, couldn't she leave him alone? George felt as if his mother had invaded the bathroom. She was standing outside the door talking to him like she was in the room right next to him. It was embarrassing. Couldn't she wait until he'd finished? George didn't answer her. If he paid no attention to her, maybe she'd think he couldn't hear her.

"George?" his mother said.

He ignored her.

"George, I've got to get started on dinner right away if I make that chipped beef thing, so which shall it be?"

Why couldn't she make up her own mind? What the hell did he care whether they had chipped beef or casserole? He didn't feel hungry anyway. George zipped up his fly and opened the bathroom door without flushing the toilet or washing his hands. If she had noticed that, it would really get to her. She was a nut on cleanliness. No luck. Her mind was still on chipped beef.

George brushed past his mother. "Won't be here for dinner. I've got to go out. I'll have something later when I get back."

His mother turned and followed him back down the hall. "George, that's twice this week you've missed dinner. I wish you weren't involved in all this basketball practice and whatever else it is you are doing. They keep you just too busy."

Before her words were even finished, he imagined his father saying, "George, you've got to keep after sports. But of course you have to keep up your grades, too. High grades— that means a better college. Sports—that's what makes a man. Why, when I was in school I . . ."

George shook his head to clear out the memory of his father's "when I was your age" stories.

His mother was still following him down the hall. "George, you remember what your father said about doing the lawn. Now he meant it when he said he wanted it done this week.

Today is the last day of the week. You better do that before you go."

George kept going. He grunted "Bye, mom," swung open the door, and gave it a shove to make it bang behind him as he jumped off the porch. He heard his mother opening the door and assumed she was looking out after him as he went down the drive. He didn't turn around. It helped his anger just a little to know she was staring after him and he wasn't looking back.

Adolescents need their parents but do not want to be treated as children. By rebelling against their parents, withdrawing from them, or denying their value, they may convince themselves they are more like adults than children. However, rebellion, withdrawal, or lack of valuing do not signify children's maturity to parents. It may be helpful to parents to recognize that when adolescents do things parents may not have let them do in childhood and do not want them to do now, it may be that the adolescents are not so much rebelling against their parents or rejecting parental authority as trying to distinguish more between their childhood self and their adolescent self. Having adults to talk to other than their parents may be very valuable to adolescents at this time. The parents of friends, a clergyman, a teacher, an understanding relative may all be able to help them define how different they are from the children they once were. They also may be able subtly to help adolescents grapple with what truly distinguishes adults from children.

Once around the hedge and out of sight, George slowed down. What the hell was he now going to do? He didn't want to go to Brodie's. As much as he liked Brodie, he was probably out working on that car of his and George just couldn't find any interest in doing that right now.

He was too angry to go over to Marilyn's house. Marilyn wasn't too sympathetic to his angry moods. The last time he'd gone over there when he was feeling mad, it was a disaster. She had started pestering him about a record she wanted him to buy her for her birthday. They'd gotten into a big fight. God, she was so bossy. At least she could let him decide what he was going to buy her for a present! Anyway, it had taken them two weeks to make up. No, he'd better not go to Marilyn's—he didn't want to have to go through that again.

Besides, Marilyn's mother wasn't too keen about their seeing each other on week nights. George often wondered how Marilyn's parents really felt about him. Marilyn's parents were high-class people. Her father was medical director of the hospital, which made them rich and respected. George got the feeling he was tolerated like a rental car—a temporary necessity until they found the right car to buy. That put pressure on him, in always feeling he had to make himself more of a somebody in the eyes of Marilyn's parents.

"Oh, hell," George thought. Sometimes he just felt so damn uncomfortable being alive. From the outside he was sure people thought he was doing fine. After all he was popular and got good grades and was on the basketball team. But inside he knew something was wrong. He was always just near the point of busting. Like something inside of him didn't fit anymore. But it didn't fit the outside world as he knew it either. He wanted something to change. But he didn't know what. The only security he seemed to have was if things stayed the same, and yet that was intolerable. At times like this, he felt so alone. "God, I'm weird," he thought.

Some teens are suspicious of mental-health professionals because they are not sure what mental health is or what mental illness is. They are concerned that their individuality will not be recognized. Essentially, mental-health professionals recognize that each person is an individual with the capacity to grow, to know him- or herself, and to make choices that will develop his or her potential.

Therapy (treatment) given by a mental-health professional can help people remove obstacles to growth, and free them from attitudes and behaviors that limit their lives and undermine their freedom and independence. Mental-health professionals do not cure *people or do something* to *them. Rather, they are trained guides who help individuals explore the limitations they impose on themselves and help them gain greater control over their own lives.*

George kicked at a crumpled empty cigarette pack someone had thrown on the ground. "Anyway, I'm not going to spend my time worrying about all that now. I'll just figure out some place fun to go and get away from all this. He felt in his jeans pocket. A buck seventy-five. Not even enough for a movie.

His pace slowed. Then suddenly he turned and quickened his walk. Why not? Everyone else did it. Donnie's house. Of course. Now where the hell did the kids say it was? Oh yeah. Some place off Brewster on Kensington. Yeah, that was it. A yellow house with a big doghouse on Kensington.

It took him about thirty minutes of brisk walking to get to Donnie's house. Donnie answered the door himself. His parents were divorced. His mom was a nurse and George knew she had the three to eleven evening shift. Nevertheless he asked, "All clear?"

Donnie looked a little surprised, then he smiled. "All clear," he said. "The house is mine. C'mon in."

The boys moved toward Donnie's room in the back. Donnie glanced sideways at George. As far as he knew, George didn't go for the stuff. As a matter of fact, a lot of the guys who were in sports either never did it or swore off during the season. The coach always laid his terms out straight so the players knew what he expected and what he'd do if they didn't follow his line. His line was "No alcohol, no drugs."

As soon as they got to Donnie's room, Donnie went to the closet and reached up a high shelf for a shoe box. "I've got it in here. I keep moving it, though, since I can't have my old lady finding it. I've hidden it so many different places, sometimes I forget where I had put it. Once I hid it so good it took me three whole days to find it. What a bummer that was."

George looked down at the marijuana in the box. There was a lot of it. George wondered where Donnie had gotten the cash. Donnie always seemed to have enough for himself and friends. Maybe he was dealing. Brodie had once said he thought Donnie sold to middle-school kids in the county school system. But it really didn't matter to George what Donnie was into. He had come for the stuff, not to be friends with Donnie.

Donnie rolled one and they lit it up. George wasn't as good at smoking as Donnie. But he watched the way Donnie did it and soon began to relax. A nice mellow feeling came over him. Donnie got up from where they were sitting and turned on the radio. The music was great. George heard it as he had never heard it before. They grinned at each other and smoked some more.

Adolescence is not just a phase one manages to "get through." It is an important time in which thoughts, feelings, and experiences all combine to lay the foundation for adult life. In using drugs, the adolescent is avoiding an important psychological opportunity of adolescence—that of testing out and adjusting his developing self-identity as an adult with the real world.

———————

George began to wonder why he and Donnie had never become friends. They were in the same grade at school. Donnie was certainly a great person. Besides he was terribly funny, or at least it seemed to George some of the things Donnie was saying and doing now were really funny.

Finally George said, "Look, I've got to go. My dad is going to ground me for a week if I don't cut the grass." He paused. His last words sounded very funny to him. "Cut the grass," he repeated, laughing as he did so.

Donnie stood up. "Oh, don't cut the gr-as-ssss," he said, making a scissors motion with his hand somewhere near the reefer.

George stood up. "But I got to cut the grass." He did a little step to music as he said it.

"Oh, cut de grass, cut de grass," Donnie started singing and turning around in his own dance step. "My friend Georgie gotta cut de grass."

"Gotta get off my ass, gotta get out and cut de grass," George danced down the hall into the bathroom and dropped the roach into the john and flushed it. "Cut de grass, cut de grass." He waved, dipped, and turned to the music and then danced through the living room to Donnie's front door. "Off my ass, cut the grass," he said, dipping once more and moving sideways out the door.

Donnie stood in the hallway by his room grinning after George. The last thing George saw before the front door closed was Donnie taking a farewell drag and blowing the smoke in his direction.

George turned and started down the porch steps. "Off my ass, cut the grass," he hummed as he did a fancy up and down movement on the stairs. However, something went wrong with his perception and he missed his footing and went flying down the steps, arms flailing. He came to a rest on his side on the grass.

George lay still a minute, then grinned and rolled over on his stomach. A blade of extra tall grass was waving about three inches from his face. George tried to narrow his eyes into a steely glint as he had seen in the movies. "Nobody's going to laugh at me like that," George said through clenched teeth.

Slowly he moved an arm up alongside his body without taking his eyes off the tall blade of grass. Then finally, with what was intended to be lightning speed but was, instead, something of a slow wavering motion, George grabbed the blade of grass around its "throat" and pulled it out of the ground.

"Gotcha," he said, rising slowly to his feet. "I told you I'd get you for that." Then as suddenly as his interest in the blade of grass had appeared, it disappeared. George danced off, his hand unconsciously opening, leaving the blade of grass to fall unnoticed back onto the lawn. "Off my ass, cut the grass," he hummed and started for the Johnsons'.

When he got to the Johnsons', he was surprised it was getting dark. He must have been at Donnie's house longer than he realized. As a matter of fact, he had a little trouble getting Mr. Johnson to understand that he definitely needed to borrow the lawn mower that night, coming darkness or not.

Finally George started up the street toward his house with the lawn mower. His face wore a broad grin. Everything was so deliciously smooth. The fading light looked particularly unusual and pretty to him. Once he veered off the sidewalk into a tree and had to back the lawn mower away before he could push it on. Who put that old tree there? he thought, his smile widening.

He arrived at his house and pushed the lawn mower into the center of the yard. It was gas-powered and Mr. Johnson had said it was low on gas. George went into the garage and brought back the gas can. He had trouble keeping the gas opening in exact sight so he spilled a fair amount of gas on the lawn. Eventually he figured that enough must have gotten in. He'd better have gotten enough in; the gas can was now empty.

He took the can back to the garage. "Off my ass, got the gas, cut the grass," he hummed. He did some fancy steps to this tune on the way back to the mower. Then all of a sudden, he stopped. The mower had taken on the shape of an animal. He tried to make out the bold letters on it. T O R O. Of course, why hadn't he noticed earlier it was really a bull.

George aligned himself with the machine, keeping a safe distance from it however. He pretended to hold out a red cape. "Hah, hah, Toro," he called, waving his imaginary cape. Then he twirled, pretending to let the cape trail magnificently behind him as he turned. The lawn mower sat in the center of the lawn.

George was up on his toes holding the cape out again. "Hah, hah, Toro!" he called, waving the cape. Again he imagined the bull passing by him as he neatly turned. He looked back at the lawn mower. It was so quiet. It would be better if it were making noise.

He walked over to it. "Hah," he cried as he pulled the starter rope. The rope slipped out of his hand. Nothing happened. He grinned.

"Hah," he cried as he pulled again, but his powerful jerk turned out to be only uncoordinated yank. He began to laugh. He tried again but couldn't get it right. He was laughing so hard now he had to sit down next to the lawn mower. Finally he was able to stand up and tried getting it started again. The first time he pulled, it threw him off balance and he spun around. The next time, miraculously, he got it going.

Harooommmmm. The noise seemed extra loud in the rapidly closing quiet of evening. Harooommmmm.

George planted his feet squarely behind the lawn mower. Now he was the bull. He pushed the start lever of the mower and charged off across the lawn. He was angry. He was chasing a stupid man holding a cape. He wheeled around and charged back. As he turned, the mower gouged out a piece of sod. Vrooommmm. He gave the mower even more power. Vrooommmm. He turned and was off again chasing across the lawn.

Suddenly a faint light lit his arena. He became aware of someone yelling at him. It was his father standing at the doorway. He had the porch light on.

"What the hell are you doing?" his father yelled.

"You said if I didn't cut the grass today, I'd get grounded, so I'm cutting the grass," George yelled back.

His father's next words were muffled by the sound of the lawn mower as George wheeled it around and started back across the lawn.

"What?" George yelled, stepping up the motor speed again and making another turn.

His father yelled something but when he realized George was neither hearing nor answering, he made a disgusted gesture and went back into the house.

Out of the corner of his eye, George watched him go. He slowed the bull and moved it over to an unmowed area. This time he didn't rev the motor so much. Instead he carefully moved the mower and scripted the word "Dad" in the grass. It was getting so dark he couldn't quite see whether it had come out all right or not. But it really didn't matter. He knew it was there.

Then he moved the bull down to the end of the lawn and turned back toward the writing. "Hah," he yelled, and reving the lawn mower, he sent it grinding right through where he had written. "Toro!" he yelled, turning the mower quickly, but he ran it back across the same area with such force and speed that he overshot the edge of the lawn. He realized it was too late; daffodils and tulips were being cut up and petals were flying all over.

He backed up the mower, turned, and started diagonally across the lawn. Best to change directions. He made two more trips back and ran into the hedges. God, how did I do that? he wondered as he again backed the mower out, leaving some broken branches behind. Finally he couldn't see the lawn in the dark anymore. Surely it was all cut. Besides he was tired.

George fumbled to shut the lawn mower off and managed after a couple of tries. He left it sitting in the middle of the lawn and went into the house.

Jeez, am I tired, George thought to himself. Without saying anything to his parents, who were in the den watching television, he went to his bedroom. He fell into bed without taking off his clothes.

Somewhere in his dreams, George saw a green-colored horse. The mare had her head down in a beautiful meadow and was eating tulips and daffodils. George climbed a fence to get into the meadow. He wanted to see if she would let him ride her. But just as he got close, the mare lifted her head. It was then that he realized it wasn't even a horse at all but a bull. The bull's eyes were fiery red in its slick green body. It snorted and lowered its head to charge.

George tried to run but couldn't. He stood horrified. The bull was coming closer and closer. George could see murderous hate in the bull's eyes. He tried to scream. But no sound came out.

Just as the bull impacted against him, it fell apart. It was made of green grass cuttings which showered over George, getting into his mouth, ears, and nose. In the cuttings were bugs—leggy crawly things that began running all over him. George began twisting and turning, swatting and kicking, and beating furiously at the hundreds of bugs.

Gradually he began to wake and realized he was kicking and striking furiously at the covers. He sat up. He was hot and itchy and shaky. What a bummer. He got out of bed, pulled off all his clothes and then lay back down on the bed naked. What a bummer.

Wonder what made me dream that crazy thing, he thought. He tried to go back to sleep but ended up lying awake. Mid-semester tests were only a week away and he hadn't turned in his science project yet. Pressure was on for the last two basketball games. He had to think of somewhere he could afford to take Marilyn this weekend that she would think was neat. Then there was his dad. What new lecture would he give George this weekend? George rolled over. The hell with everything. Oh, the hell with it all.

One should not minimize the stress adolescence places on individuals. Adolescents who cannot tolerate authority when others can, who are poor achievers in contrast to their potential, who are consistently depressed or who threaten suicide, who go from "high" to "low" without any intervening leveling off, who rebel to the point of harm to themselves or others, who have poor relationships with others, who show intensive, unrelenting anger over minor irritations, who demonstrate unusual fear in situations, who take extraordinary precautions to prevent things they think will happen, may all benefit from some kind of mental-health evaluation to determine if these are passing behaviors or behaviors that would profit from mental-health intervention.

2

Is This the Way It's Always Going To Be?

MARTIN

Martin felt miserable. It was all over school what had happened with the girls. It had been a week now and everyone was still laughing at him. No one would listen to his explanation that he was finding out when the gas gauge showed the tank to be empty. Instead all they talked about was how Martin had picked up a load of girls and purposely ran out of gas.

"My God, anyone of us would like to run out of gas with Jennie Brock," Peter Dunkin, one of the most popular guys, had commented loudly in the locker room after gym. "But to run out of gas with six girls! . . . Martin, you must think you really are a super stud. Wham, bang, thank you m'am! Now it's your turn, sweetie. What was your name again and what number are you? I've lost count."

Everyone had roared with laughter. Martin felt humiliated. He didn't even date and Peter's alluding to his making it with all those girls embarrassed him. Martin tried to hide behind his locker door, but guys kept walking by making remarks like: "Hey Martin, next time you decide you want to get down with that many girls, better get yourself a station wagon!" and "Hey, hey, what'd you say, we thought good old Martin was gay—But right before our very eyes, he turns out to be a super stud in disguise."

27

Even when he walked down the school hall, Martin got comments or, worse yet, giggles and stares. He had thought of getting sick and staying home for a couple of days, but he was afraid his absence might become an excuse for more jokes. So instead he brazened it out as much as he could during the day. At the end of school, he tried to hang out in someone's classroom long enough to avoid walking home at the same time the other kids did. Lucky he didn't have to take the school bus.

Today Martin had stayed after class to talk to his English teacher, Miss Nutter, and was grateful she seemed as pleased as he was to talk. In due time, however, she indicated she had some work she wanted to finish up. Martin felt enough time had passed anyway, so he thanked her and headed for the side door. By accident, however, he arrived at the school door almost the same time as Jennie. She had her cheerleading uniform on a hanger in a plastic bag. She didn't see Martin come up behind her as she opened the outside door. A torrent of rain made the cement steps outside almost invisible.

"Ohh," Jennie said and shut the door quickly. She backed up and stepped on Martin's foot. "Oh, I'm sorry," she said, turning quickly. Then as she recognized Martin, her tone changed. "Oh, it's you," she said.

Martin's mind raced for just the right thing to say but he couldn't think of anything.

Jennie went to the door and opened it a crack. Small bits of water pelted at her. "C'mon, mom," Jennie said half out loud. "I'll get my uniform and my hair ruined if I have to walk home in this rain."

"Is your mother coming to pick you up?" Martin asked before he decided if that was really what he wanted to say. Immediately he wished he hadn't said it.

"She was supposed to if she didn't have to work late," Jennie answered without turning her head to look at him. She opened the door a crack again. "C'mon, mom," she pleaded.

"Look," said Martin. "I'll be glad to go home and get my car. I don't live all that far from here and I could be back in about ten minutes and drive you home."

"Martin, I've had one of your rides already," Jennie replied sarcastically.

"No," Martin hastened to assure her. "That was just an experiment. Really, I'm serious. It wouldn't take long to get my car and I could drive you home."

"C'mon, mom," Jennie said again, ignoring Martin and opening the door a crack to look out.

"Seriously," Martin said, edging past Jennie and taking hold of the door knob. "Look, I'll be back in ten minutes. If your mom hasn't come yet, I'll give you a ride home."

Jennie was forced to step back. She looked at Martin curiously as he turned up his jacket collar and prepared to open the door.

"Well, thanks, Martin," Jennie said. Then she went on, "But I don't know for sure my mom's not coming. She should be here."

"Well, I'll come back just in case she doesn't." Martin slipped out into the rain. It was stupid to go out in such a downpour, but this was his chance to make it up to Jennie. Maybe it would get some of the kids at school off his back too. He hurried on through the rain going either at a half trot or a half run depending on the number of puddles he had to navigate around.

Martin was sure the car would be at home. His dad never drove to work and although his mom drove to work most of the time, she didn't drive on Wednesdays. Wednesday was her night to work late. After dinner, his dad would take the car and pick her up since she didn't like to drive home late by herself.

Sure enough when he turned the corner, Martin saw the car sitting in the lot. He ran into their apartment and grabbed the keys. Normally he would have taken off his jacket and changed his shoes since they were soaked. However, he was anxious to get back to Jennie. He left the apartment quickly and jumped in the car.

Every minute seemed like five as he started driving back. What if her mother got there first? That would ruin everything. What if someone else like Peter Dunkin happened by and gave Jennie a ride? He grimaced at that thought and tried to drive faster.

The rain was coming down in torrents. Martin had a hard time seeing as he drove. Then with a guilty start he remembered to check the gas tank. It was okay. There was over a quarter of a tank left.

Martin finally turned the last corner and pulled up in front of the school. He slid over into the passenger's seat and looked hopefully up at the school door. The next time it opened he could swing the car door wide open and motion Jennie to run down the steps and get in. The school door didn't open. He stared at it so long that once he imagined it had opened a crack and then closed. But then after a couple of minutes when no one came out, he realized it must have been his imagination. The rain was coming down so hard it had probably distorted his vision.

Finally Martin decided he'd better get out and go in. Maybe she wasn't waiting at the door. Maybe she had gone back to the office to try to call her mom. Maybe she was wandering around the building trying to see if anyone else was there who could give her a ride.

Martin moved back into the driver's seat and took the keys out of the ignition. He turned up his jacket collar. It felt cold and wet on his neck. Gathering himself for a sprint, he ran around the car and up the steps. The minute he opened the school door he saw that the spot where Jennie had been standing was empty as was the hall.

Hopefully, he went toward the school office but found the

lights had been turned out already. He went quickly through the rest of the building. Miss Nutter was still in her room but Martin didn't want her to know he had come back to the school so he went quietly by her door.

Martin finally had to face the fact that Jennie was already gone. He felt a terrible sense of disappointment even though he had known it would probably turn out like that. He went slowly back to the school door where they had stood just twenty minutes before. Martin pushed the door open and shuffled back down into the car.

He didn't turn on the motor right away. Instead, he sat thoughtfully. The rain pelting down on the windshield completely obscured his vision. The rest of the windows were steamed so he could hardly see out anywhere. He was blocked off from the rest of the world.

What if Jennie had gotten in the car? What if he had started driving her home? What if he turned on the radio to get some music? What if the music had suddenly been interrupted by a flash-flood warning? What if there had been a *tornado* warning? Martin imagined the look of horror on Jennie's face and what might have happened after that . . .

"Martin, there's a tornado warning! It's not just a watch! It's a warning! That means there's been one spotted and it's heading our way! How far are we from home? What should we do?"

"We're too far from your house to try to make it, Jennie. I'm going to make a run for the bridge. If we can drive down to the creek under it, we'll be safe."

"But what if . . ." Jennie protested.

"It's the only chance I've got to save us, Jennie," Martin interrupted, patting her hand reassuringly.

Jennie looked at Martin with admiration and gratitude. She knew she was dependent on his skill as a driver to get them there before the tornado struck. Martin gunned the motor and shot off. Everywhere trees were falling from the force of the wind and the rain. Martin skillfully dodged them until he came to a place where two trees had fallen across the road, their topmost branches entangled, making a barricade.

"Martin, we can't make it! Our way is blocked!" Jennie shouted.

"Don't worry, Jennie, you're with me, remember? And if anyone can do it, I can."

Martin shoved into second gear and stepped on the gas. The car shuddered as it ran into the branches and then seemed to grit its tires and churn forward. As the branches scraped the paint from the car, there was a tremendous screeching which sent shivers of pain through Martin's teeth. Still the car continued to lurch forward through the tangled tree limbs.

Martin finally felt the car begin to slow as it fought valiantly to push through the branches.

"Martin, we're not going to make it," screamed Jennie.

Martin shoved the car into first gear and pressed harder on the accelerator. Suddenly he saw where to the left a larger limb was broken. At the last minute, he turned the wheel and the car jerked crazily into that part of the tree. Jennie reached over and clung to Martin.

Martin yelled "C'mon baby!" to the car. The car strained, then the branch was shoved aside. Martin felt the car's rear wheels push forward. Suddenly they were free.

"Martin, we've made it!" Jennie said, and excitedly kissed him on the cheek. Then suddenly she let go and turned. Both of them could hear the roar of the tornado in the distance.

"Martin, it's coming!" Jennie screamed. "It's too late."

"Don't worry, Jennie. I can save us," Martin yelled. "The bridge is just ahead."

With great skill Martin shot the car forward. But there was a giant muddy hillside ahead before they would be safe under the bridge.

Martin had to start down much faster than he wanted because the roaring behind was getting louder. If they flipped over, all would be lost. The car was sliding crazily. Martin took his foot off the accelerator and jammed on the brakes. Nothing happened.

"Damn!" he said. "The brakes are gone. It must be all this water."

"Martin!" Jennie screamed. "What will we do?"

"Don't worry," Martin said. "I'll use the handbrake." With one hand on the handbrake and another on the wheel, they slithered down the hillside. Martin worked the wheel furiously, righting the car two times just before it was about to roll over. At the last minute he applied the accelerator and gunned the car into a perfect parallel position under the bridge.

At that moment there was a giant roar—like a freight train—as the tornado whirled overhead. Jennie grabbed Martin and held onto him. He put his arms around her and pulled her against him. They held each other as they listened to the steel and concrete on the upper part of the bridge being torn apart. Was Martin right? For a minute he doubted his wisdom. Would the bridge hold or would it be ripped away so much that the rest would come crashing down on them?

Then, almost as quickly as it had come, the tornado winds were gone and there was nothing but the sound of the rain beating on the stream.

"Oh, Martin," Jennie said, almost fainting in his arms. Her eyes closed for a moment but when they opened, they were full of adoration. "Martin, I'm so lucky to have been with you. I would be dead otherwise." Then she pulled his face close to hers and kissed him long and tenderly. He tightened his embrace and began to kiss her back. He moved to get into a better position when suddenly he was aware of a strange sound. It was a roar in the distance that was getting louder.

Then Jennie heard it too. She broke off their embrace. "Martin, what is it?" she asked.

Martin listened intently.

"Is the tornado coming back?" Jennie cried nervously.

"Shhhh," Martin said.

"What is it?" Jennie asked again.

"We've got to get out of here!" Martin said. He switched on the ignition and began rocking the car back and forth by shifting first into reverse and then into first in an attempt to free the car's wheels from the mud.

"Martin, what is it?" asked Jennie.

Martin didn't reply. He was intent on freeing the car. Suddenly he looked up. "It's too late. Hold tight, Jennie. Here it comes," he yelled.

Jennie looked out the window in time to see what Martin was staring at. It was a wall of water higher than the car, coming toward them down the normally placid stream.

"Martin, what's happening? What is it?"

"Dam must have broken upstream," Martin answered.

Just then the water hit. It washed over the car as the car waddled crazily in the muddy gouges its tires had made deep in the stream's bed. The water picked up the car and the next thing Jennie and Martin knew, they were floating crazily on top of a torrent of water.

"Martin, we're floating away!" Jennie cried both in relief and in horror.

"Yes," said Martin. "That's one thing about these old foreign cars, they built them a lot more solidly than new American cars."

"But how long will the water stay out?"

"Not that long. See, some is seeping in now. But I think I can help." Martin ripped off his jacket and shirt and stuffed them alongside the cracks at the bottom of the door and around the place where the brake, clutch and accelerator went into the floor. "Quick!" he yelled. "Take off some of your clothes and stuff them along the bottom of the door on your side."

"Martin!" Jennie seemed shocked as she looked down at her pretty sweater and skirt.

"Here!" Martin grabbed Jennie's cheerleading uniform, which she had in a plastic bag, and jumped in the back seat and started shoving it around the doors in the back. Then ripping away the bottom cushion, he stuffed more clothes along the edge of the seat where it met the trunk.

"Now, get out of those clothes!" Martin yelled.

Jennie obediently took off her sweater and skirt and shoved them around her door. Martin finished packing the back.

He then climbed back in front. Although he had seen beautiful lacy underclothes like what Jennie wore in the Sears catalogue, he had never seen them on a real person before. Especially someone with beautiful soft skin like Jennie's. Martin stared for a moment. He felt himself rising to the occasion. But then a lurch of the car as it was spun around in the water made him turn away. He had to somehow get the car under better control. The packing wouldn't keep out the water forever, and he had to have a plan of what to do next.

Suddenly he yelled, "Get the screwdriver and pliers out of the glove compartment!" He jumped into the back seat. He turned its cushion completely over. "Now quick, hand them to me!" With lightning speed, he ripped off the material covering the frame. He unbolted the longest piece of the metal frame. "Okay," he said. "Now when I get out on the roof of the car, you hand this to me."

"Martin, it's so dangerous!" Jennie said. "Please don't!"

"Don't worry, baby, I can make it," Martin said.

He rolled down his window and climbed out. As he did, the car tipped dangerously and some water sloshed in from the open window. Martin almost lost his grip on the top of the slippery car.

"Martin!" Jennie screamed.

Martin hung precariously for a moment and then hauled himself up on the roof. He lay down, spreading his weight on the car so that it righted.

"Now hand me up that piece," he yelled.

The car continued to be spun around in the surging water. All kinds of debris were floating alongside it. The car tipped dangerously in the water as Jennie handed up the large piece of metal. As Martin grabbed it, it almost slipped away. Slowly he brought it up to the top of the car. Fortunately, his dad still had the car-top carrier on so Martin had a place to brace his feet and hips as he sat up and brought the piece of metal into position.

Martin lined up the piece of metal between his feet and lowered it over the back of the car into the water. He strained with every muscle not to let it slip. Then facing backward and looking over his shoulder, he began to use the piece of metal as a giant rudder.

"Look out!" he heard Jennie shouting from the car. Martin steered with his rudder and barely avoided the car's slamming into the corner of a building that was half submerged in the water.

Next he . . .

Knock, knock. A tap at the car window startled Martin. He straightened up in his seat and with an embarrassed look rolled down the window. When he did, he saw Miss Nutter peering in at him.

"Are you all right, Martin? I looked out the window and saw a car here for the longest time. I thought maybe someone had run out of gas."

Martin cringed and shot a quick glance at Miss Nutter. Gas? Was she making fun of him too? But it was obvious from the expression on her face that she was serious. She must not have heard about the other incident.

"No, Miss Nutter. Everything's fine. I was just going." Martin started the motor. The rain was dripping off Miss Nutter's umbrella into the car on Martin. "Do you need a ride somewhere, Miss Nutter?" he asked without a great deal of enthusiasm.

"No thanks, Martin. My car's over there in the parking lot. I was just going home and thought maybe I'd first better check who was in this car. Well, drive safely and I'll see you tomorrow."

"Okay. Bye, Miss Nutter." Martin rolled up his window and pulled away from the curb slowly. When, ten minutes later, he pulled into the apartment parking lot, he found he didn't remember driving home. He had been busy working on his dream about Jennie and the tornado. When he got into his apartment, he hurried out of his wet clothes and into a warm tub of water. Then he continued with his dream, rewarming the water whenever it began to feel cold.

Martin was still sitting in the tub about two hours later when his dad got home.

Adolescence is a time when young people are likely to engage in daydreaming or fantasies. Fantasies are actually helpful to adolescents in that they give them an opportunity to mentally explore and sort out their real and imaginary lives. This includes all kinds of fantasies, including sexual ones. Sometimes young people feel guilty about their thoughts and need to be reassured that even seemingly bizarre fantasies can be within the range of normality.

LYDIA

"Lydia, what's the matter?" Cecilia caught up with Lydia as she started down the school steps.

"I just can't stay today," Lydia said.

"Are you sure there's nothing I can do?" Cecila put her hand on Lydia's arm.

Lydia's eyes watered a little. "No, but thanks."

"This is the fourth time you've cut school since you've been back," Cecilia called after her. "Be careful or they're going to suspend you."

Lydia knew Cecilia meant well. Actually it was nice of Cecilia to care. Cecilia came from a family with all kinds of problems and Lydia knew Cecilia was having a tough time herself keeping her life on an even keel. But Lydia's friends and what they thought didn't matter that much anymore.

Right now Lydia didn't care what the school did. She didn't care if they suspended her or even kicked her out.

Lydia had seen Wayne with his new girlfriend today. She had been walking down the hall when all of a sudden she became aware he was just a little ahead of her with his arm around his new girlfriend. Lydia had stopped right where she was. The hurt was so great she thought she would cry out on the spot. Instead, she had just turned and started toward the door.

Deprivation, stress, unhappiness, and emotional shock can bring about mental illness. People who are more vulnerable than others can deteriorate under the strain. Experiences, both recent and long past, clearly have a lot to do with mental illness. Other factors, such as economic hard times, body chemistry, and genetic inheritance may all play a role.

Lydia paused, wondering where to go. She really couldn't think of anywhere. There was nowhere to go, nothing to do. Mechanically, she turned her steps toward home.

But home was not going to be comforting. Her mother still acted as if the feelings Lydia had for Wayne were those of "puppy love"—as if they didn't matter very much. But they hurt beyond belief. They did matter. Lydia felt as if Wayne was the only meaningful person in her life. He was the only one who had really seemed to like her for what she was as a person, who had wanted to get to know her better and better.

Lydia's mother couldn't even guess at what Lydia and Wayne had shared. Lydia had told Wayne things she had never told anyone else. She shared her feelings about lots of the kids at school. She told him about her father, her mother's divorce, her dislike of her brother and stepsister, what her dreams were for the future. She told him about what it felt like to be a girl, to be in love, to care about someone like him.

And her mother couldn't possibly know what she and Wayne had shared physically. Even though it was against her upbringing and she had been frightened and ashamed at first,

Lydia had been having sex with Wayne. Lydia did not find sex very satisfying herself but she wanted desperately to please Wayne. The fact that he wanted her was very meaningful to her. Knowing she was sharing herself physically with him made their relationship seem more complete. Lydia, deep inside, also felt having sex with Wayne would make the relationship more lasting.

A young person who feels a great desire to be loved may have sexual intercourse as a way of becoming close to someone. Having sex may also be an attempt to find security in a love relationship, although, too often, in young love relationships the security may not become a reality or may be shortlived if it does. For some young people, having sexual intercourse can also be an attempt to replace a parent of the opposite sex with a substitute love-object. There are other reasons for why young people have sex, including lack of strong societal supports for postponing sex as well as peer pressure toward having sexual intercourse.

Lydia felt her mother had no idea of the kind of love Lydia had experienced. Although she knew her mother loved Jim, all they ever seemed to talk about were taxes, food, the house they'd like to build, his job, her job, local gossip, "the kids" (as they called Lydia and her brother and stepsister). It was not the least bit romantic and she couldn't imagine they ever shared any real passion. It was a more superficial love than the love she had for Wayne. It was shallow. It was humdrum, dull.

A terrible heaviness came over Lydia. Was Wayne having sex with his new girlfriend? Was he looking at her the way he used to look at Lydia? Was he kissing her the way he used to kiss Lydia? Was he saying the same things to her he used to say to Lydia? Did everyone at the parties look at his new girl and treat her in a special way because she was Wayne's girl, just like they used to with Lydia?

These thoughts created a pain almost more than Lydia could bear. She continued to hurry away from school. When she got home, she was surprised to find her mother's car in the drive. Then she remembered her mother had said she was going to stay home and finish up a special report for the management of the company she worked for. Lydia went in the front door and went directly up to her room. Her mother was busy at the desk in the living room and didn't see her.

Lydia lay down on her bed. If only she had a knife to cut out the pain. She dug her fingernails into the palms of her hands hoping the pain of having her nails cut into her flesh would stop the pain she was feeling inside. But it didn't. She pressed harder. This time the sharp cutting of her nails distracted her temporarily. But the minute she relaxed the pressure, the pain inside her welled up and overcame her.

"Oh, my God, no! My God, no!" she cried, burying her head in her pillow.

Lydia didn't know how long she lay crying and moaning before she realized the phone was ringing. It rang several times. Finally she heard the front door open as her mother came in hurriedly from the outside.

"Hello," her mother said. "I'm so sorry. Could you repeat that? I'm out of breath. I was down the drive getting my mail when I heard the phone ringing and ran back to the house . . . Why no, Lydia's not here. She's at school . . . Are you sure? . . . No, she hasn't come home . . . No, I didn't know that she had been missing school. I thought she had been going . . . Yes, I will surely check into it . . . Yes, thank you for calling. I'm sorry you had to do it."

Lydia heard the receiver click down on the holder. Then all was quiet. Lydia envisioned her mother sorting through the mail and then getting back to the report she was writing.

Lydia put her head back down on the pillow. She didn't want to go to school. She didn't want to do anything. She just wanted to stop feeling, to stop hurting. Maybe she wanted to die.

All of a sudden, the door to her room opened. Her mother said in a surprised tone, "Lydia, you *are* home! I didn't know you were here! Someone called from school a little bit ago and I told them you weren't here!"

"How come you're not at school?" Then her mother noticed the redness around Lydia's eyes. "Oh, dear," she said, going to put her arms around Lydia. "What's the matter?"

"Mom, leave me alone, please," said Lydia. "Please, mom, just go." Lydia pulled away from her mother.

"But, dear, I just want to help. What's the matter?"

"Mom, I said, just go!" Lydia's voice was rising.

"But, dear, it's not like you to miss school and I want to know . . ."

"Mom, just go!" Lydia screamed. "Go! Go! Please go!" She turned her head and began sobbing.

Her mother stood up, stared at Lydia for awhile, then turned and left.

Lydia heard the door close. She was relieved her mother had gone back downstairs, yet it reinforced her loneliness and emptiness. She continued to sob. "I just can't go on like this," Lydia thought. "I can't stand the pain. I can't take it. I just can't take it. I can't stand people staring at me, looking at how I feel—at school, at home. And I can't stand any questioning. No one can possibly understand. They aren't me. They can't feel what I feel. I just want to die."

Lydia got up and went to the bathroom. She opened the medicine cabinet. Maybe there was something there she could take. Something that would put her to sleep so she wouldn't have to feel the pain, wouldn't have to face anyone's questioning of her.

Lydia knew people killed themselves by taking more pills

of one kind or another than they should. She stared at the bottles in the cabinet. There were antiperspirant, mouthwash, toothpaste, prescription medicine from when Finney had an earache, laxatives, and a bottle with four aspirins left in it.

No, there really wasn't anything there powerful enough to give her the relief she sought. What it all meant was that the pain was going to go on. This very minute she was going to have to go back down the hall to her room with the pain still there. She was going to have to endure it as she lay on her bed. She was going to have to endure it when it was suppertime and she had to go downstairs and eat dinner with her family. She was going to have to endure it while the family watched television that evening. She was going to have to endure it when she went to bed.

Lydia didn't know whether she was glad or sad there was nothing in the cabinet she could use to cause her death. Maybe she would get something lethal tomorrow. She didn't know for sure. It was just that right now she couldn't stand the pain.

The loss of a meaningful relationship can be the trigger for a suicide attempt by a depressed adolescent. In some cases the adolescent may not really wish to die but rather to obtain relief from his or her feelings. For example, an adolescent who takes pills may be longing for a deep peaceful sleep free from dreams rather than the finality of death. In other cases where the adolescent sees his or her life as being more hopeless, the meaningful relationship may have been the only force that allowed the adolescent to tolerate pain or the problems in his or her life. Some attempts at suicide by adolescents are not real attempts to die but rather a bid for attention, in essence a cry for help. Some adolescents, saved from their suicide attempts, express sorrow at their act. They really do want to live, and resolve never to try again. However, if the problems that caused the adolescent to seek suicide as a so-lution remain unresolved, the resultant stress may lead to another attempt. All threats of suicide should be taken se-riously.

GEORGE

George got up and went into the bathroom. He squinted in the mirror. He knew he was fairly good-looking—that was one of the reasons he'd been able to get Marilyn. He was tall—that was one of the reasons he was okay in basketball. And he was pretty smart—that was one of the reasons the science teacher was on him. If they knew you were "college material" (weird they called it that, like you were this mold-able blob), they bugged the life out of you.

George knew his high school, which was known as a good one, had a reputation to keep up. The way the kids scored in the S.A.T. didn't just affect whether or not they got into college, it affected how the school was ranked. And how the school was ranked affected how property values in the school district were rated. And property values affected prices people could get for their homes and who could buy into their area. It was a whole rat race. So the science teacher was bugging George not because he cared about George but be-cause he wanted the school to look good and property values to stay up and the whole rotten mess. Jesus, it made George so angry just thinking about it.

George stared into the mirror without seeing. It never ceased to amaze him. Here Russia and the United States had enough super-powerful bombs to blow each other up ten times over. Moreover, from what George could tell, the idiots on both sides believed that a super-bomb war was winnable. But people didn't seem to care about the lunacy in the world. All they thought about was property values and not that the whole world might be blown up and there wouldn't be any property left. George hated grownups. They were so self-indulgent and stupid. They never cared about anything really important. They filled their lives with petty tasks and when they weren't being cruel to animals or each other, they were just plain dull and boring. Boring, boring, boring. George sometimes was so bored he just couldn't stand it.

George's face came back into focus in the mirror. Oh well, he wasn't going to worry about all that now. He took his time finishing up in the bathroom. Now where could he take Marilyn at night that he could afford and that she would think was neat? George still hadn't decided when he wandered into the kitchen for breakfast. Saturday and Sunday were the only times the family generally had breakfast together. Sure enough everyone was at the table. George took one look and knew something was up. Everyone had serious, drawn expressions on their faces. Even his stupid mixed-up sister who usually appeared serious looked more somber.

George debated whether or not to say anything and decided against it. He felt he would soon find out anyway. He took his place at the table and reached for a piece of toast. Before his hand closed on it, his father began. "George, you are grounded for two whole weeks. And if you ever do anything like that again, I'll ground you for a year!" His father's voice rose with every word.

"Grounded for what?" George immediately became angry. "For what? I mowed the damn lawn like you said."

"You mowed it, huh?" His father's voice rapidly got louder. "Mowed it, huh? Well, you go look." His father half rose out of his seat in a threatening way. "Damn it, you go look right now!"

"Dear," George's mother turned to his father, her super-sweet voice trying to soothe him.

"You keep out of this, Mildred," his father retorted. His angry stare came back to rest on George.

George shrugged, got up out of his chair, and went through the house to look out the front window.

"Jeez," George uttered automatically at what he saw. He blinked twice and then just stared. The lawn was incredible. It was almost as if a tornado had hit it. Some parts were mowed and some parts weren't. In some places it appeared to be dug up. Small clods of dirt and grass were scattered here and there. The flower beds in two places were all chewed up and there were muddy tire tracks leading to both places. In one case, the tracks led into the neighbor's hyacinth bed.

"How did I get way over there?" George thought in amazement. Then he noticed the bushes under the living-room window. Some had broken branches. One was even uprooted.

"Shit! I don't remember doing that," George thought. Yet there was no doubt in his mind that it was all his handiwork. "Well, I'll be damned."

George was pensive. Then he vaguely remembered playing bullfighter and bull. A smile darted across his face. Donnie would just split a gut when he found out about all this. His smile broadened. Donnie would probably think this was the funniest thing he had ever seen. He really had to call that guy up and have him come see it. George was turning to go to the phone when his father came in.

"As you can see, it's the work of a six-year-old gone berserk," he began. "I'd just like you to know that I can't for the life of me figure what got into you, but if you ever do it again I swear I'll ground you for a month and I'll . . . ."

"Okay, dad," George butted in angrily. "You said it. I've heard it. Okay? Now just back off. I did it. And you've laid down your precious penalty. So back off, huh."

"Don't tell me to back off," George's father stepped toward him. "Don't tell me to back off when you've done something like this! You're the one to back off!" He was waving his finger in George's face now.

"Listen, son, and you listen good. As long as you live in

my house, you don't tell me to back off. This is my house, and my yard, and you don't tell me to back off." His father was working himself up even more. George could see he was searching in his mind for something more powerful to say.

Finally George's father said, "And that grounding includes the basketball game. No game next Saturday night."

"But dad," George blanched. He didn't think his dad would do that. Not his dad who bragged about his son on the basketball team. George was sorry he'd talked back. "Dad," he pleaded. "Please, not the game. Honest. I'm sorry I did it. Look, I'll go out and cut the rest of the grass and fix the flower beds. Please. Look, it's the next to the last game. I gotta be there."

"No," his dad said. "No! You don't touch my lawn again. And you don't play in the game. That's final."

"But, dad," George started to plead.

His father's voice rose in triumph. "Back off," he said with a smirk.

George wheeled around and plunged toward his room. Anger swelled up in him. He wanted to explode. His father had him and he knew it. God, he hated his father. He hated being sixteen. He wished he were grown and out of this house, out from under his dad, his mother, and his stupid weird sister. God, did his dad really know how much it hurt being nearly a man but being treated like a little boy? His father had him. There was no way he could even try to sneak out and play the game. If the coach ever found out he'd disobeyed his father, he'd be off the team and all teams for the rest of this year and maybe next year, his senior year, too. The coach was a nut on discipline and obedience, regardless whose rules they were.

George felt terribly down from his despair and yet strangely up from his anger. He slammed the door to his room. His mind raced over what two weeks coming straight home from school and staying in would do to him. Oh God, Marilyn.

He remembered their date tonight and the fact that he had promised her a special treat—that they would go someplace really neat.

Yeh, some treat. Some really neat place—nowhere. And he wouldn't be able to see her next week after the basketball game. He winced. If he felt really secure about her, it would be different. But he really didn't know what two weeks of not seeing her would do to their relationship.

Damn his dad. God, this could really mess up his life and it was his father's fault. The guys on the team would be upset he wasn't there to play. In basketball you practiced to be a team, to be a machine, and a substitute part in the machine meant the whole team had to be that much more alert, play that much better and harder, because it never was quite as good with a regular out.

Sure he had messed up the lawn but it was his father's fault for not understanding what grounding a guy for a game would mean to them all. The guys would resent that he'd screwed up and had to miss the game. They had an outside chance for the playoffs—a real outside chance but it was there. Damn. George slammed his fist into the pillow on the bed and then sat down. Unexpectedly, a sadness came over him—so strong that for a moment it competed against his anger. George felt the turmoil inside as the two emotions battled it out.

Finally, both feelings tempered enough for George to begin to think other thoughts. He had better make his call to Marilyn as early as possible. Postponing it wouldn't make it easier. He didn't want to stand her up at the last minute. This way maybe she could find some girls who didn't have dates to do something with. She wouldn't like that but he knew she'd be less grumpy about things the next time he saw her if she'd at least gone someplace tonight rather than stayed home.

After his call to Marilyn, George felt angry again. At first she'd seemed nice about it, but toward the end of their conversation he noted a different tone in her voice. Maybe she too had begun to realize more fully what two weeks' grounding meant. Then just before they'd said goodbye, she'd made a remark about how glad she was to be going steady with him—how it made her life so exciting because she never knew what she could count on. That had done it for George. He managed to control his temper just long enough to hang up.

Girls. Jeez, everyone dated. Only the kids who weren't anything didn't date. God, he just had to date. But dating took so much time, he thought. So much time and thinking had to go into relationships. Of course, he liked the feeling of having his arms around a girl, maybe even being able to explore her body with his hands, and dreamed of the time when it would work out and he could get really close to her, even have sex with her. But, God, it took time. You had to date but it took so damn much time.

George thought again about the basketball game, about having to come home every day like a baby. The more he thought about it, the more he wanted to strike out at something. Then he had an idea.

George checked to see where everyone was in the house and then went to the phone and lifted the receiver. He didn't want anyone accidentally picking up on his conversation.

On the third ring, Donnie's mother answered the phone. "No, he's not here. I'll have him call you when he gets home."

George put down the receiver. He was beginning to get excited. He decided to go back and stay in his room for at least the rest of the morning. He unplugged the extension phone and took it to his room and plugged it in there. It would be easier to talk to Donnie in his room. Furthermore, he really didn't relish running into any member of his family for a while.

He thought about what to do to pass the time till Donnie called. Well, he might just as well finish that science project. He had it partly done anyway. All he had to do was finish the model he had started and then write it up. That way, the science teacher would get off his back. Besides, he had a nice reward coming later on. He got his materials out and began working hard.

George had just about completed his project when the phone rang. He picked up on the first ring. "Yes, this is George," he said. "Need a favor. I want two weeks' worth." Donnie's reply showed the surprise George had expected. "No, I mean it," George said. "I'm grounded for two weeks including the basketball game." To Donnie's response George replied, "No, it wasn't because I didn't mow the lawn; it's because I *did* mow the lawn. Look, when you come, you'll see it and you'll understand."

An hour later, Donnie arrived at the front door. "George," his mother called. "Donnie's here with something he says you need to finish your science project . . ."

"Thanks, mom," George said, hurrying from his room to the front door. Over Donnie's shoulder, George could see his dad on his hands and knees trying to fit some of the clods of grass back into the lawn.

"Jeez, I see what you mean" was the first thing Donnie said. "Did you do that?" He had a smile of wonderment on his face as he said it.

George answered, "I guess I did." The remembrance of his bullfight came back to him once again and he smiled too. "I sure must have liked your stuff."

"Well, then, here's the stuff you need for your science project," Donnie said in a loud straightforward voice, handing George a bag. Then he lowered his voice, "And remember I get your new letter jacket in return. You promised."

George looked around before he said in a low, annoyed tone, "Of course, I promised, didn't I? Look, I'll bring it to school Monday. There's no way I can give it to you here."

"Sure," said Donnie, Then he said admiringly, "Boy, when

you cut de grass, that's not all you cut. Wish I could have been here to see you do it."

George smiled again. "I knew you'd like it. See you Monday. I can't ask you in. You understand. It's part of the grounding."

"I understand," Donnie said, turning and starting down the steps.

"Monday, man."

George shut the door. As he started back to his room, his mother called to him. "George, you didn't have any breakfast, don't you want some lunch?"

"Naw," said George. "I'm anxious to finish my project. Just call me when it's dinnertime."

The whole family was amazed how calm George seemed at dinnertime. His father's frequent references to the mess on the lawn didn't even seem to phase him. He just responded politely or didn't answer at all. Even when Geraldine, his sister, started babbling about how someone really had it in for her (which usually drove him up the wall), he remained calm.

His mother remarked later to his father that maybe it was getting the science project done that had made such a change in George at dinner. She commented that George always seemed to be under a lot of pressure about something.

George's father replied that is was no more pressure than he had had when he was young. In fact, it was a great deal less, and then he launched into one of his "when I was young" stories. George's mother had probably heard it fifty times before, but she listened in her pseudotolerant way as if she was hearing it for the very first time.

3

Turning On, Turning In, Turning Out

MARTIN

Martin sat down at the dinner table. His mother was already seated and was staring politely at her food. His father was reading the evening paper and had not yet come to the table.

"Martin, I'm not sure I'm going to be able to eat this," his mother began feebly.

"Sure you can," said Martin. "Don't worry. I froze the bottom part of it so it won't be defrosted till you get down to it. That way the tastes don't run together. Besides, even if they do come together a little bit, it all gets mixed up in your stomach anyway."

"But isn't this a bit extreme to avoid having to wash dishes?" his mother asked, a great deal of doubt still showing in her voice.

"It's not just a work-saver," Martin explained, "it's economical. It also saves on dish soap and water. You see, if you use actual food as your dishes and silverware, there is nothing left to wash so you save on time, soap, and water. Plus it's more sanitary."

"See," Martin went on, "you use the celery as a spoon." He picked up a nicely washed piece of celery and pointed to the broad end. "And you use this carrot as a knife. See how

52

I've pared it down into a wedge-shaped blade. I froze it to make it even harder. I got three knives out of one carrot," he added.

"I'm not sure I could cut steak with it," his mother said, picking up her carrot knife.

"We never have it anyway," Martin quickly admonished her. "We can't afford steak."

"And this is the fork," he went on. "It took the longest to make, but I'm sure I'll be able to do them faster next time." Martin looked proudly at the strands of cooked spaghetti he'd neatly twisted into the shape of a fork and then frozen to make it stiff.

"When's dad coming? We better start to eat before our forks melt."

"Oh, you know how hard it is to get him to the table once he's started reading the paper. I don't think he'll mind if we start." His mother started to add "He might even be grateful," but then thought better of it. Instead she said, "Now explain to me again. Exactly what is this?"

"Well," said Martin enthusiastically, "I used a watermelon slice to make the plate. I left most of the watermelon on it so that that will be the fruit dessert when you get down to it. Don't worry, though, I froze the watermelon so that it will stay cold even though it has a hot dinner on it. See, I lined the top of the melon with a little bit of bread so that the hot spaghetti wouldn't exactly be resting on the melon. Then I put the spaghetti on one half and lettuce with a bit of salad dressing on the other."

I see," said his mother with as much interest as possible. "Now what do I do first?"

"First, you eat the spaghetti and bread liner with your spaghetti fork. Then you eat your salad with your carrot knife and spaghetti fork. Then you eat your spaghetti fork and carrot knife. Then you eat the watermelon with your celery spoon. Then you eat your celery spoon."

His mother gulped a little and looked down at the steaming spaghetti nestled next to the salad on the watermelon slice.

"So it's not only practical, it's nutritious," added Martin, digging his spaghetti fork into his spaghetti enthusiastically. After two trips to his mouth, however, the spaghetti fork had thawed out and hung limply from his hand. Oh well, he would just use the celery spoon with his carrot knife as a pusher. He dug in again.

At this point, Martin's father joined them and Martin explained all over again what a nutritious, economical, time-saver, cost-saver dinner he had invented by having edible silverware and dishes.

"You mean, I've got to eat the watermelon rind?" his dad asked.

"No, that part's not edible but it doesn't have to be washed, it's disposable," Martin explained.

Martin's dad cast a glance at his mother and then tried to pick up his spaghetti fork. He found it was already too limp to use.

"Just use your celery spoon and carrot knife," Martin said. "I've got to think of something else for a fork." Martin dug in eagerly again.

"My salad's a little warm," his father commented, having decided it would be safest to test the lettuce and dressing first.

Martin noted the spaghetti had slopped over on the salad a bit. But then the watermelon slice was not as big as a regular plate. "It must have been the spaghetti that got on it," Martin commented.

"Oh dear," Martin's mom stood up quickly, brushing at her lap.

"What's the matter, mom?" Martin asked.

"I think there's some water running out from my melon," she said.

Martin looked over at her watermelon slice, then at his.

The water was coming out of his too, and was nearing the edge of the table. He popped up and got a dish towel. "Here, dam it up at the edge of the table," he said, taking a swipe at his water and passing the towel to his mother. "The spaghetti must be melting the melon faster than I thought it would. Maybe next time I ought to scrape the watermelon out and put it on top so you eat that first."

"Watermelon on top of my spaghetti?" Martin's father asked, struggling to get some spaghetti to stay on his celery spoon.

Martin noticed the difficulty he was having. "Yeh, we do need a fork for the spaghetti. I really got to work on that."

"Martin, would you mind if I got a plate and slid it under my rind?" his mother asked. "Just this once until you get it perfected?" she added.

Martin sighed. He was disappointed they couldn't finish the meal as planned. Messing around with dishes would defeat his whole purpose. He sighed again and said, "Oh, okay."

His mother got up.

"While you're up," his father added hastily, "would you get me a fork?"

Martin shot a quick look at his dad. It really wasn't impossible to use the celery spoon and carrot knife. He at least could have tried a little longer.

Martin's mother returned to the table carrying three plates and three forks. She handed a plate and fork to his father and kept one set for herself. She pushed the remaining set toward Martin. "Do you want to use these?"

Martin shook his head no. Determinedly he lifted more spaghetti onto his celery spoon. By the time he got down to his melon, however, his spoon was no longer very stiff and his carrot knife-blade broke off as he tried to cut into the watermelon. The water from the melting melon was dripping down onto his pants. He did the best he could in getting at some melon and then ate his knife and spoon.

"Well," said his mother eating the last of her knife and

spoon. "At least I only have two plates and two forks to wash after dinner. That's a big improvement." She said it as positively as possible as she sensed Martin was disappointed.

Martin looked troubled. "There's also the spaghetti pans," he said. "I made the salad in them before I cooked the spaghetti, so I didn't dirty a salad bowl." Then he added, "But I couldn't figure out what kind of thing there was you could eat that you could also cook the spaghetti and the sauce in. Most things would burn up."

His father gulped as an image of a watermelon sitting over the gas burner came to mind. "I'm sure that's why the folks who can afford them have dishwashing machines. Just because they can't figure out how not to do those pots," his father said.

Martin looked at his father to see if he was serious or making fun of him. But Martin couldn't tell by just looking at his father. His father was kind of a quiet man and Martin never quite knew what he was thinking.

"Well, anyway," Martin's mother said, "this dinner was a very novel idea and certainly a unique experience."

Martin looked at his mother. The conversation was not exactly making him feel terrific.

"Yeah, well," said Martin, getting up. "I'll help clear the table." He carried his watermelon rind to the garbage bag. It gave him a sense of satisfaction as he dumped it in. At least his dinner had resulted in no dishes. His parents put their rinds in the bag too and their plates and forks in the sink. His mother took a sponge and began wiping the remaining watermelon juice off the table and floor.

"Want me to help with the dishes, mom?" Martin asked.

"No, dear," his mother said. "I think it was great you made dinner for us. You just go and start on your homework."

Martin nodded and went to his room. He had shared the room with his brother for so many years it still seemed strange to walk in it and find no one there. He still missed his brother too. They had been quite close. But Harold had been in the Marines over a year now, so Martin had the room to himself.

Martin lay down on his bed. He felt really down. Funny he had been so up and excited while he was working on dinner and now here he was with a kind of emptiness.

Adolescents are subject to mood swings, which often makes it difficult to assess an adolescent's emotional state. All adolescents are subject to occasional depression. When, however, it is the primary mood overall even though the depression comes and goes, there is reason for concern. Some depressions may be related to irregular maturation. Some adolescents grow away from their childhood self without being able to replace it with a firm, growing, adult self. They therefore feel empty and doubt whether they can really feel. In other cases, attempts at resolving personal growth issues may have been met with continuous failure. Their environment may not be a nurturing one. In such instances, in order for adolescents to be able to grow to an adequate adulthood, mental-health intervention may be necessary.

Lots of time he had that down feeling at school too. For example, he could walk around with crowds of kids everywhere and still feel empty and lonely. But he wasn't really unhappy so it didn't make a lot of sense.

Martin knew he wasn't one of the popular kids. Yet he couldn't say he really wanted to be popular either. He didn't feel he had much in common with popular kids. A lot of what they talked about didn't interest him in the slightest. Martin liked what went on inside his head best of all. But it wasn't anything that he could expect to tell anyone else about. Sometimes he felt as if he was separate from his body, like he was a person tucked away inside an outer shell. He could even feel that inside person staring out through the openings that were called eyes. He'd look down at his hands and arms and consciously make them move just to satisfy himself that the person inside could control the shell in which he lived.

As adolescents move toward adulthood, they must become adjusted to their new body form. Adolescents respond to new physical sensations as well as familiar ones with different awarenesses of body and self. They begin to form a new self-image. Stereotypic models of ideal womanhood and ideal manhood often make it hard for adolescents to feel confident about their changing bodies. Since the size and contour of their bodies may not conform to the ideal, they have doubts whether their new bodies will function in an ideal manner.

Mental health and body health are interrelated. Some mental-health problems may have physical signs such as skin rashes, ulcers, and headaches. On the other hand, hormonal imbalance can cause psychological changes. Compulsive eating leading to obesity, excessive dieting to achieve thinness, overconcern about the body leading to hypochondriacal behavior, all may indicate there are problems that need to be addressed through mental-health services.

Martin stared at the ceiling vacantly. "I wonder about me. Sometimes I really wonder about me." Then almost as if it were really happening, he heard the principal's voice saying over the school's public address system—

"**Students. This is a proud moment for Ronald Reagan High School. As you know, the world has been facing a severe energy crisis. But one of our very own students has made a major contribution to solving it. And today,** in a formal ceremony inaugurating the worldwide campaign for meals with nature-made disposable dishes and edible silverware, we will all be having our lunch in . . . coconut shells."

Martin smiled to himself—that would at least solve the freezing-melting problem. Maybe you could cook in them too—he wasn't sure. He'd never had coconut except on a birthday cake at a party he'd gone to in the fifth grade.

"Now there will be TV camera crews at the school all day," the principal was saying, "so I want everyone to be at his best. A real vote of our admiration goes to Martin Bannerman, who made this important event come to pass."

Jennie was sitting near the window in Martin's first-period class. The sunlight streaming in glanced off her dark hair, making it gleam. She turned admiringly to Martin, who was sitting on the other side of the classroom. He saw her pass a note across the room to him. It had to go through Peter Dunkin. It was clear that Peter was jealous of Martin getting a note from Jennie.

Martin opened the note and read it: "Martin, you are brilliant. I consider it a great honor to know you. Would you like to meet me after school and come to my house to listen to records? I'll be waiting. Fondly, Jennie."

Martin closed the note and looked across at her and nodded. But as he did, he saw a man's face appear briefly in the school window behind her and then disappear. Martin's heart leaped into his mouth. It was what he'd been dreading.

Martin's plan to save on the energy, water, and soap needed to wash dishes had unintentionally eliminated the need for mechanical dishwashers. The big corporations had warned him that if he carried out his plan to introduce the world to edible plates and silverware, it would mean a multimillion-dollar loss to them. The loss of the dishwasher business would be so serious for them, they warned him, they'd "get him."

Of course, Martin didn't back down before them so now they had a contract out on his life. The man in the window must be the person they had sent to kill him. His mind raced. The bell had just rung. Jennie had already gone out of the classroom. He would not be seeing her again before the end of the day. If he met her after school as planned, that would endanger her life. If he didn't meet her, she would think he didn't like her.

In his mind, Martin skipped briefly over the TV cameras and the ceremony at noon and got to the part where school was just over. Martin decided he would have to disappoint Jennie and started to go home by a different route. But Jennie had caught sight of him somehow. Just as she caught up to him, he saw "the man" aiming a gun at him.

"Quick! In here!" Martin yelled. He shoved Jennie into the TV van that was still parked outside the school. Luckily the keys were in the ignition. Without hesitating, he switched on the motor and spun the van into action.

"Martin!" Jennie screamed as a hail of bullets peppered the back of the van, smashing the rear window and shattering some of the expensive TV equipment inside.

As he pulled away, Martin could see in the rear-view mirror the TV camera crew running out of the school door. He could also see "the man" getting into his own car and spinning after them.

"Martin, what is going on?" Jennie asked in terror.

"No time to explain now." He looked over at her. "Look, I'm sorry I got you into this, but don't worry, I'll get you out of it . . ."

Martin stepped down on the accelerator. He took a corner on two wheels.

Martin's mother was saying to his father in the living room, "You know, Martin is such a bright imaginative boy . . . I mean he's always thinking up unusual things, doing different things. It's a wonder he doesn't get better grades in school."

His father, who was watching a news program on television, just grunted.

"But then maybe his thoughts just don't fit with the regular things they teach in school."

"Uh huh," his father said absently.

"Sometimes it worries me though," his mother went on. "Martin doesn't show any interest in girls. He doesn't seem to have many boy friends. Don't you think that's a little odd for a boy his age?"

"Why?" his father said.

"I mean," his mother continued. "I'm not sure at times that Martin is normal."

"Well, he doesn't have to be like everyone else," Martin's father said and continued watching his program.

"No, he doesn't have to be like everyone else. But I do want him to have a happy life and be well adjusted. He really doesn't seem to do very many exciting things like I remember my brothers doing at his age."

Martin's father didn't answer.

Back in his room, Martin was just lighting a stick of dynamite and saying to Jennie, "If my throwing arm is as good as it used to be, I'll have us out of here in no time. When I throw it, be prepared to duck. Okay, now DUCK!"

Adolescence is a very important time of life. Many adults prefer to look at adolescence as just a phase "to get through"

*instead of recognizing how important it is to life's process.
These adults do not wish to recognize, perhaps, how important their own adolescence was to their lives. This may lead
them to underestimate the significance of providing appropriate mental-health services to adolescents in need of them.*

*Normal adolescence encompasses the sorting out of thoughts,
feelings, and experiences so that they become the basis for
unity upon which to build adulthood. When this important
process becomes blocked, the adolescent would be best served by
mental-health intervention. However, the mental-health
professional working with the adolescent should be someone
whose training has prepared him or her to work with developing patterns rather than working primarily with the
amelioration of past unhealthy development. With the support of a mental-health professional, the adolescent thus is
enabled to decide what from his or her childhood can be kept
to serve him or her in adulthood and what should be let go
as being no longer useful.*

LYDIA

Lydia paused a minute, shading her eyes. The rocky dirt road
curved around the brown ocean hillside, now appearing, now
disappearing. To the right lay the ocean crashing and pound-
ing playfully at the rocks. Somewhere up ahead, the road was
supposed to lead to a small beach. She had no idea how far
it was. But going to the beach gave her a small purpose,
somewhere to go, something to do. She started walking again.
The strangeness of this drab stone and earth world constantly
reminded her she was in a different land.

If Lydia had not been so sad, she would have smiled at
how she had tricked them all—her family, her Aunt Milly,
the cab driver who spoke hardly any English. Her Aunt Milly
and Uncle Ted had recently bought a small villa on the ocean

in this foreign country as a retirement investment. They had been told it would make them a lot of money, because in the next ten or fifteen years this remote sleepy community would turn into a bustling ocean resort. There were already signs of change. The only grocery store had wooden doors sagging open at odd angles to the dirt street. It had no refrigeration and the items on its shelves were limited mostly to canned goods and a few packaged items. In great contrast, at the end of the street, there was a Dairy Queen with bright umbrellas over painted tables serving lemonades, cokes, and dairy whips.

Her Aunt Milly, who lived in another city, had wanted Lydia to join her and her uncle on their visit to the villa during the summer. That was what the call to her mother and the mention of a passport had been all about. But subsequently, Lydia had succeeded in intercepting letters and placing two confusing telephone calls that enabled her to be here all by herself during spring vacation. For Lydia the school vacation just made it possible to leave home. She had no idea whether or not she would ever be going back.

All adolescents have secret feelings, attitudes, and behaviors they may not choose to share with others. However, there are adolescents who hold on to privacy to an abnormal degree. For whatever reason they cannot share or seek help from anyone. On occasion, these adolescents solve their problems in a private way and move on to a fairly healthy adulthood. However, those who cannot do so by themselves may find their personal growth limited and their adulthood unfulfilled.

Lydia continued on her way. The day was growing rapidly hotter despite the cooling breeze from the water below. The road passed beneath a few houses high on a hill. These were not like the big rich villas along the road at the edge of town.

These were small gray shacks. There was no sign of life around them. Their wooden fences, aged and sagging because of the sun and wind, spoke of the poverty in this land. Brown, tan, weathered chalk—the landscape had no color. It had no life.

Then a tiny object on the road, like a bright red pumpkin seed, caught Lydia's eye. She looked closer. It was a bug. Its black short legs moved ever so slowly. Where would this small part of life be at the end of a day for all its moving? Her shoulders sagged. Where would she be at the end of the day for all her moving? She thought if only she could understand this bug—its relationship to her tortured self—maybe she could escape some of the pain. Somehow it seemed as if between them there must be some kind of answer to life. However, that answer, like all the others in her life right now, seemed just out of her reach. Reluctantly she turned away and started walking again. Her legs moved on, carrying her with them.

Lydia didn't think of Wayne as a person anymore. His body form was hazy in her mind. What she thought of was the burning rejection, the aloneness, her lack of purpose for being. At times, she wanted to enter herself with a sword, to slash and try to destroy whatever was life inside her.

Lydia had seen pictures of fires set to fields in Africa. They burned whatever was in the fields to the ground so that the soil would be plantless and fertile in time for the next crop season. Maybe that was what she had to do—destroy everything left inside her so that something new could grow.

But the pain, the emptiness, the desolation racked her body day and night. Here at least she was away from the grinning cheerful faces who could never understand what was going on inside her. Here she could look at rockiness and desolation. And here she could look at the barren landscape as if it were herself turned inside out and search it for solace and meaning.

She entered one of the many "U's where the cliffs swung

in and out. The inside of the U was shaded and its cool was welcome. However, its somber contrast to the burning brightness of the sunny road brought out more of her sadness. She walked on.

Lydia had been walking since before seven in the morning. As she came out of the U, in the distance she saw the coastline reappear, somewhat hazy in the heat and stretching endlessly before her. It was nearly ten. If a person could walk about three miles an hour, she had gone at least ten miles. There was no way to tell where the beach might be. "If I'm not there by noon, I'll just turn back," she thought to herself. But going there was something to do, to accomplish. She quickened her step.

Time passed. The U-turns in and out along the ocean seemed endless. She watched the waves splashing over and over the rocks below her. The wind occasionally blew mist from the jumping waves against her face. She continued walking around another jutting curve.

Suddenly, there was the sound of a car behind her. As she stepped out of the roadway to let it pass, an old pickup truck rattled alongside her and stopped. The door opened. Inside sat a dark-haired man dressed in sun-faded clothes. A little boy sat next to him, peering out curiously. The man motioned for her to get in. She shook her head no and smiled. He motioned again to her and said something pleasant-sounding in Spanish. She waved her hand and shook her head politely. "It's a nice day. I'd just like to walk."

Lydia could tell by his expression he didn't understand her. The child still stared curiously. Again she smiled. "No. Thanks, no." She added a "Gracias" in the best way she could.

He shrugged, smiled, reached over and closed the door. The truck roared off. Lydia turned to avoid breathing in the billowing dust. It was then, facing the direction from which she had come, that she saw there was nothing left of the villa, the town. It all looked strange; curve after curve had shut her off from everything recognizable. Her lip trembled and her eyes clouded. But that was the way it was. All that she had was with her right now. The present obscured the past. Inside her was a stranger searching for some small new beginning.

Lydia turned and started again on the road. The truck had already disappeared around the next curve. The morning air was heavy now. The ocean breeze had died. She tried to walk a little faster although the stones in the road made walking uneven.

Two more turns. Three. Five. Then Lydia gradually became aware of rhythmic sounds somewhere ahead. Chink. Chink. Chink. With each curve her curiosity grew. At last, rounding an outer turn, she understood. Below her lay a magnificent inlet. On the inside curve by the water a giant stone hotel was rising. The chink, chink came from tall wooden scaffoldings on which hundreds of hammers and trowels were being used to lay stones and bricks.

Lydia paused. The road led between the partially completed hotel and the rugged cliffs. She felt alone and very vulnerable. If it had not been for her desperate pain, she never would have had the courage to fly to the capital, change planes and fly to this unknown town and her aunt's and uncle's tiny villa. She never would have had the courage to find the caretaker in town in the morning and convince him to take her to her aunt's villa and give her the key.

Until now she had felt safe staying here. Her aunt's villa was only a five-minute walk from the tiny town. There were few people in the town and to Lydia they all seemed quiet, uncurious, and concerned with their own lives. Lydia had wandered around the town into the grocery store to buy some canned food, to the Dairy Queen for a dairy whip, to the end of town to watch people leading burros with packs on their backs, and to the town's small square where people occasionally spread blankets on the ground and sold cheap plastic items or aluminum cooking utensils, without anyone's having paid much attention to her.

Now, however, she remembered she was a young teenage girl, walking alone in a strange country, and no one knew she was here. There were so many people in the inlet. She had no idea that there were that many people in this part of the country. Where did they all come from? Where did they all live? They were not from the town certainly.

But if she wanted to go forward, there was no other way to go. Until now, she had allowed her hat to hang down her back by its cord. Carefully she pulled it up to her head, drew the brim forward and adjusted the cord. After another hesitation, she took a deep breath and started forward.

At first she heard only a few whistling sounds. Maybe it will be all right, she thought. But as she walked, the whistles began to multiply and she knew they were directed at her. She concentrated on the road ahead—how much farther to the center of the U, how much farther back out again.

Calls and wails added to the whistles as more and more men working on the scaffolds became aware of her walking on the inlet road. The sounds grew until the inlet itself became a giant male throat swelling with lustful noises. The steep rugged hillsides picked up the sounds and sent them back amplified a hundred times over. Lydia felt a sense of panic rising in her. She wanted to cover her ears and run.

Instead she kept her even pace. She was now in the center of the U next to the rising hotel. The cacophony was overwhelming. She saw bodies moving suggestively on the scaffoldings and felt hundreds of eyes watching her.

Lydia caught her breath. Whatever she had felt about the loftiness of mankind was now gone. She saw humanity as reduced to a base animal, driven only by primal urges. Yet she felt reduced too, reduced to a survival level inside herself. She had come here to survive. Her going someplace today was a mere gesture to keep alive, to survive.

Tortuously she wound around the base of the U, her grief first holding off and then bending under the weight of the sounds. Finally, she began to climb up the other side where the road led out of the inlet. Even then, however, the calls and whistles reverberated off the hillside, mercilessly pursuing her.

At last she reached the outer curve and rounded it. She saw ahead a new view of the ocean and a stretch of cliffs beyond. The breeze was fresh on her face—a small rebirth. As she wound her way around the hills, she was aware the chink, chink, chink had resumed behind her.

Lydia flipped back her hat and moved forward with a new energy. Two more turns, three, five. She glanced at her watch. Her heart sank at the thought of turning back. Yet it was past noon and she still had not arrived at the beach. How much further to go? She didn't want to give up. She had walked so far. But it was time to turn back. She decided to try one more bend, then another. Still no beach. She couldn't deny she was worried. She had been walking for about six hours. Yet she had to get there. She would try rounding just one more hill.

Suddenly she heard a motor car. She stood aside. A battered-looking taxi was coming toward her. Maybe it was the same one that had brought her from the distant airport to the small town. Several people hung out the windows and waved and called to her as they went by. "They have to have been coming from the beach," Lydia thought. "It must be just ahead."

Lydia quickened her pace. Another turn of the hillside and still no beach. But then the hillsides were becoming a little less steep. She sensed she was close. Another turn and, yes, there it was—a flat land recessed into the hills and an inlet of shallow water. The scruffy grass also made it different from the other inlets. Two cars were in the dirt parking area where the road ended. As she drew closer, she saw a woman with two children on the sandy beach and a man lying in the sun in one of the grassy areas.

Lydia walked gratefully down to the water, took off her shoes, and began wading. The water was warm and sparkling. For a brief while, her pride and pleasure at having achieved her goal made her unaware of the pain inside.

———————

Even people who are well-adjusted are not well-balanced at all times. Emotional upsets during adolescence are quite common because the transition from childhood to adulthood is not an easy, smooth process. It is natural to be nervous before an examination, to be upset when plans to do something important do not work out. The loss of someone the adolescent cares about can be extremely upsetting. The well-adjusted person recovers from disappointments and unhappiness while the emotionally unhealthy person doesn't.

———————

GEORGE

George leaned back in his seat in chemistry class. It was one whole month since the grass-cutting incident. Somehow his two weeks of pleasure had turned into a month of pleasure. Like right now. The teacher was saying something, but all George saw was the beautiful play of the ceiling lights on the glass test tubes and beakers. There were so many new perspectives looking at things through a drug haze. He just relaxed and felt good about everything.

———————

Another way to stay mentally healthy is to find a way to deal with pressure. Some people try to deal with it by turning to alcohol or drugs, which only creates more problems. Emotionally healthy people find healthier outlets. They may try new physical activities—hiking, running, swimming, tennis. They may develop new interests—learn to play a musical instrument, learn photography, volunteer at a hospital or daycare center. They may develop new skills—woodworking, needlecraft, repairing toys or small appliances. These activities help people to work off anger and frustration, or permit them to focus their attention on things they can relax with and enjoy. Some people need to take a further step if the stress in their lives becomes excessive. They may have to evaluate the number of commitments they have and weed out the ones that are less necessary or less enjoyable. Students may have to cut back on the number of extracurricular activities or cut down on the number of hours spent in an after-school job. Not everyone can handle the same amount of pressure, and reduction of the amount of demands and stress in their lives may be the only solution for some adolescents.

The bell rang. George noted the interesting quality of the bell's tone—a stretched-out sound made of several individual notes rather than just one harsh clang.

He rose slowly and ambled toward the door.

"Just a minute, George," the teacher's voice was sharp behind him. "George, what's got into you lately? You used to be one of the better students in this class. But your midsemester exam was terrible. You're doing sloppy work now and you don't seem to care. George, what's brought about this change in you?"

George listened. "I'm trying, teacher, honest I am," he answered slowly. "It's just that, well, you know, basketball practice and all that."

"Basketball season is over, George," the teacher said.

George suddenly remembered that the teacher was right. He didn't have basketball practice anymore. "Well, you know,"

George added, "you still gotta practice to stay in shape for next year. And baseball is coming up."

"But we don't have a baseball competition at this high school," the teacher reminded George, looking at him curiously.

"I know," George said, searching his mind for a logical answer, "but Stavros Electrical does."

"Stavros Electrical?"

"Yes," said George proudly. "My uncle works at Stavros Electrical Supply Company and they have a softball team for their employees and they compete with a lot of other companies. And my uncle, he has to stay in shape."

"What does that have to do with you, George?"

"If he does, I do too." George smiled and reached forward. He patted the teacher on the arm and walked toward the door.

As he went out of the room, George thought to himself, "I wonder why the teacher's so interested in baseball."

"George," it was Marilyn's voice. "George, wait up! I haven't seen you all week. Where have you been?" George turned around to face Marilyn.

"Hi, Marilyn," he said. His mind groped for the right words to use with Marilyn. "Been looking all over for you," he said, thinking that that sounded good.

Marilyn started to reply. Then she stopped and looked carefully at George, especially at his eyes.

"Oh, George," she suddenly cried in disgust. She turned on her heels and walked away.

"Wait, Marilyn," George started to say, but as he raised his arm he caught sight of the movement and it was as if his arm was throwing out the words to her and he didn't need to say them. George watched the words move out, loop down like a sagging clothesline, and then reach her.

Marilyn didn't stop. The connection that was made momentarily by the rope of words was broken. The words wavered and then came back to George in a wriggly motion. George watched them till they reached his feet where they broke up and disappeared. He turned his head and started off down the hall in the other direction. "Okay," he said to himself. "Now what was I going to do? Ah yeah, I remember. On to history class." He drifted along with the other students, smiling to himself. Several students who passed raised their hands in greeting, but George did not see them.

On the way home from school, George realized that everything from history class on was a nice soft blur. He remembered falling asleep one time. When he tried to think back, he wasn't sure whether it had been in history or English. However he had managed to get through another day.

When George arrived home, his mother was standing by the door.

"Hi, mom," George said. "Home right from school again."

His mother turned, focusing her attention on him for a moment, although her expression showed it wasn't George she was looking for. "George," she said thoughtfully. "Are you all right? You know this last month or so, I haven't seen you with your friends very much. You used to be gone every minute and I couldn't keep up with you. Now you just come home and go to your room. Is everything all right?"

"Of course, mom," George replied. "First you complain one way, then you complain another. What's a guy to do?"

"I'm sorry dear," his mother said in a sweet voice. "It's just that I worry about you."

At times George was surprised his mother was never even suspicious of what he was doing. At other times he just felt secure his mom was so completely out of it she'd never guess. Plus Geraldine and all her problems took a lot of his mom's time. Almost as long as he could remember, his mom had been fussing with Geraldine—weird kid. It was embarrassing to have a sister who was so fuzzed up. He didn't know what to do with Geraldine any more than his parents did. But he wished they'd do something. The funny ways she acted and felt grossed him out, especially when his friends were around. Maybe that was why he liked to meet his friends away from home rather than have them over.

There are a wide variety of resources to turn to for mental-health services: private practitioners (psychologists, etc.), child-guidance clinics, community mental-health centers, outpatient clinics, psychiatric hospitals, general hospitals with a mental-health unit, court clinics, state mental hospitals, storefront centers. Those needing mental-health services may want to use friends, relatives, physicians or clergy for recommendations about particular services or particular professionals. Community information and referral services, telephone hot lines, an area Mental Health Association, local clinics or hospitals, may also be resources for general information about services and, in some instances, individual practitioners.

Geraldine. George frowned. The only thing was Geraldine—weird kid—might give him away. Like this morning at breakfast when his mother had said for the umpteenth time that week that she was worried about him because he wasn't eating his usual breakfast.

"Oh you don't need to worry about George," Geraldine had piped in. "George has all he needs right in his room."

"Shut up, Geraldine," George had snapped.

"I'd be careful if I were you, George. I might ask to borrow your new letter jacket or the tape recorder you got last Christmas or . . ."

"Geraldine, I'm warning you!" George had said, making a fist at her. George hated his sister. She was plain and stupid and a squealer. Plus she always had these feelings people were against her even when they weren't. And she was so up and down in her moods—really extreme.

"Children," his mother had said. "You two haven't stopped quarreling since the day you were born."

"Correction," George had said. "Since the day Geraldine was born. Everything was fine until she came along."

"George, now I said that's enough," his mother had warned. "Your father will ground both of you if he hears you quarreling again."

"Too bad he's not here to hear it," George had said.

"Yes, and I'd sure like to tell him all of it. *All of it*," Geraldine said, making a face at George.

George had gotten up from the table and stormed off to his room. He had not planned to smoke until this weekend, especially since he had been on the stuff so much recently. But Geraldine infuriated him. He just had to forget her. He turned the lock on his bedroom door and went to the place where he stashed his marijuana. There was not a lot. He really had been into it heavily lately. As a matter of fact, doing it more had made him seem to want it more. It was not that he craved the stuff itself. He craved the relief it gave him from his life. After a few puffs, he didn't care about his father; it didn't matter what his grades were this semester. It didn't matter that Phillip Symthe had gotten a car before he had; it didn't matter that Marilyn had told him she wanted to date other boys besides him—"Just once in a while," she had said. It didn't matter that he might not be able to play football in the fall because he had banged his knee up in the last basketball game. None of that mattered and that was nice, oh so nice.

So he had gone to school stoned that day. And that made school nice, so nice.

But now it was after school and George had to decide how to handle his evening.

"Look, mom," George said, "I'm going to my room to study a little bit. Call me when dinner's ready, huh?"

"Well, all right, dear. But dinner may be a little late because I have to take Geraldine to the dentist. Incidentally, you didn't see Geraldine on the way home, did you? I told her to come right home because her appointment was right after school. I wonder where she can be."

"No, I haven't seen Geraldine." George wanted to add, "And I don't care if I never do—that pest." But he didn't say it since an argument would just delay his getting back to his room.

His mother went back to stand by the door. George noticed that she had her purse and coat on the chair near the door ready to go whenever she saw Geraldine come up the drive.

George went on back to his room. He hadn't intended to smoke since he had turned on so heavily in the morning. But most of that had worn off and just a few drags would set him up nicely for the evening. He didn't bother to lock the door as he usually did since his mom was going out any minute. Besides, after rolling this one, he had so little left in his stash that it would be almost impossible to squeeze out even a half a reefer.

George sat in his desk chair looking out the window at nothing in particular, and took a puff. He inhaled deeply. He took another puff. Already he could tell the floating peace was just ahead.

Then he heard the door open abruptly behind him. He turned his head just in time to see a uniformed policeman enter his room!

———————

Drugs provide adolescents with an escape from reality. Adolescents have the capacity to experience life very intensely. The dullness of the world around them, of their own reality, may at times overwhelm them and make them yearn for escape. If adolescents choose drugs as an answer to the challenges presented them by their existence, particularly if they see drugs as the only answer, they will have difficulty developing the skills needed for creating and maintaining satisfactory and meaningful adult lifestyles.

4

What If It Gets Worse Instead of Better?

MARTIN

Martin spent more and more time making up stories about himself and Jennie. He liked his stories more than TV or movies because he was the star. He could slow down the action. He could replay the parts he liked. He could change things if they didn't come out right. He could have whoever he wanted to win, win. He could have whoever he wanted to look silly, look silly. He could have whoever he wanted to be embarrassed, be embarrassed. He had absolute power over the characters. It wasn't like real life where things didn't always go right, where everyone was so competitive, where he never got to win, where he often felt foolish and alone. In his stories he could have everything his own way.

Martin had been daydreaming ever since he was little. But now with Jennie in his thoughts, his dreams had taken on new meaning and new purpose. He started avoiding other people in order to get the quiet time needed for his daydreams. At school, he went off by himself whenever he could. If he started a good dream on the way home from school, he rushed through dinner. He lay in bed late in the morning to finish exciting parts. He went to bed early at night to continue them.

Fantasies or daydreams are not harmful in and of them-selves. They are, in fact, normal in adolescence. However, when they become so important to a young person that school, relationships with others, or activities suffer, they take on a different character. One must be alert to the fact that this may signal that the young person is having difficulty with problem-solving in real life and is using fantasies as an escape from reality rather than as a tool to deal with reality.

Young people can use fantasy constructively by imagining themselves in various situations without having to experience them. Through fantasies they can experiment with emerging cognitive skills that permit them to make choices based on alternatives and consideration of the future.

Another way, therefore, to stay mentally healthy is to not close yourself off but to keep experiencing and growing. The well-adjusted person has many interests and is involved in a number of different activities. He or she isn't fearful of trying new foods, games, meeting different people, visiting new places, learning new skills. The well-adjusted adolescent enjoys school but finds a balance between school and other experiences.

This day Martin was upset that he had to stay after school to correct his theme for English. Actually he had daydreamed in class when he should have been doing it, so it wasn't unfair. It was just that he had started such a good dream and he couldn't wait to get back to it. It was about a corrupt politician who was condemning Jennie's house so he could buy the land for peanuts. He was doing this because he knew the state was considering building a freeway there. The politician stood to make a fortune and Jennie and her family were in despair.

"Martin, pay attention to your work," the English teacher reminded him. "I need to get home and I'm sure you do too."

Martin glanced back down at his paper. Three more errors to go and then he could hand it back in. He hurried and made the last changes.

"There," he said, picking up the paper and carrying it to the front of the room.

"Thank you," Miss Nutter said in relief.

Martin decided not to go out the front door in case there were kids still hanging out on the steps. He just didn't want to pass a lot of people so he headed for the door by the gym. As he passed the open gymnasium door, however, he heard a familiar voice talking. It was Jennie's. He couldn't see her, but he paused a little beyond the door to listen. Jennie's voice sounded very unhappy.

"I told her that but it didn't make any difference."

"But," the voice of another cheerleader responded, "didn't you tell her everyone was?"

"Yes," Jennie's voice was strained. "I explained to her over and over that everyone was getting new red and white saddle shoes this year to match our costumes."

"And what did she say?"

"She just said that I'd have to figure out a way to paint the black part red because they were brand new shoes and she wasn't going to buy me another pair."

"How come you bought black and white anyway?"

"I told you I came in late the day the director talked about it, and all I heard was that we were going to get saddle shoes to wear with our outfits. I don't know why, I just assumed they were to be black and white. I don't think I even remembered they made red and white shoes."

"Are you sure you can't take the black and white ones back?"

"Yes, I asked the store manager at Potter's where I bought them and he said since I'd worn them, I couldn't bring them back. Oh, why did I have to wear them to school the next day?" Jennie wailed.

"You know I saw you with those shoes on in school," her friend responded. "I thought it was kinda funny you were wearing new black and white saddle shoes, but then I thought, 'Oh, well' and didn't say anything. I wish I had."

"Oh," Jennie moaned. "What am I going to do? I can't see why mom won't buy me another pair of saddle shoes. I'll look so funny when everyone else has red and white shoes and I have these dumb old black and white ones. And even if I got paint to paint them red, I couldn't match your color, and the paint would probably crack when I started jumping in them. Oh, I feel terrible! Why did this have to happen to me?"

Martin grimaced. His heart went out to the anguish in Jennie's voice. It was the same kind of anguish she had expressed over different things in his daydreams. This was reality though. Martin was angry at Jennie's mother for not buying her another pair of shoes. Maybe he needed to talk to her mother, explain how important this was to Jennie.

Martin paused. No. It probably wouldn't help to talk to Jennie's mother. Good saddle shoes must cost about thirty dollars. He'd never priced any. Even though Jennie's family probably had more money than his, he understood Jennie's mother. Thirty dollars was a lot to fork over twice for shoes.

"Oh, what am I going to do?" the voice sounded so bewildered and helpless.

Martin straightened his shoulders. This called for action. He moved quietly away from the gymnasium door. He looked down at the books he was carrying. They were too heavy to lug around. He went back and shoved them in his locker. So he wouldn't do homework tonight. This was more important. Then he headed off toward downtown.

By walking fast, Martin arrived at Potter's shoe store in about a half hour. He looked at the shoes in the women's window. This was a much better quality shoe store than he and his family ever shopped at. He was amazed at the prices on some of the shoes. His mother never in her life would pay $69.95 for a pair of dress shoes and yet they had some for that and more in the window.

After not seeing any red and white saddle shoes in the window, he went inside. The thought of Jennie made him overcome his embarrassment over what he was about to do.

"How much are saddle shoes?" he asked the clerk who approached him.

"We don't carry saddle shoes for men," the clerk responded. "You might find . . ."

"No," Martin hastily replied. "For women, I mean girls, you know, high school girls, girls in school activities and stuff . . ."

"Oh, you mean like the cheerleaders are wearing this year," the sales clerk remembered the red and white shoes easily, having sold five pairs in two days.

"Yes," said Martin.

"$42.50," said the salesman.

Martin blanched, "Well, uh, thank you very much."

He turned and hurried out the door. That was a lot more than he figured. He wondered why they needed shoes that expensive. Of course, he knew they jumped in them a lot. Still, $42.50 and then there would be tax.

Martin frowned. There was no way . . . Then he remembered Jennie's voice saying "What am I going to do?" He remembered the helplessness in it. She would feel terrible being the only one with the wrong color shoes. He squared his shoulders. No, somehow he had to do it.

All night Martin worried. The next morning in class he paid little or no attention to what was going on. He was consumed with the thought of getting Jennie the shoes she needed. But how? Neither he nor his family had that kind of money. He knew better than to ask his mom or dad. He drifted dreamlike along with the other kids toward the cafeteria. Sometimes he sat with a few of the boys like himself who did not have very close friends, only a few casual friends whom they saw mainly in school. One of them hurried by, waving him on, but Martin shook his head and continued to drift slowly toward the cafeteria. He had to think of a way.

Since adolescents need and benefit from peer-group support, parents can be aware of and encourage the development of relationships at an early age and into the teen years as an aid to mental health. In general, adolescents who have had a chance to form relationships with peers and others, but who have not done so, or have formed only poor relationships, would benefit from mental-health intervention.

It wasn't until he was paying for his milk at the end of the cafeteria line that it occurred to him. As he watched the cashier put his quarter in the drawer, he realized in the drawer were piles of dollars along with lots of change. It was money, lots of money.

Martin stood transfixed. Finally the cashier said, "Did you want something else?"

"No, oh no," said Martin, coming suddenly out of his trance. "No." He hurried away to find a spot by himself where he could sit watching the cashier. He saw the students file past handing her their money. It was like all the kids were contributing to Jennie's shoes. And why shouldn't they? She was their cheerleader for the school. And why shouldn't the school itself contribute? They were the ones who had the cheerleading team. Didn't they have a responsibility to see that the cheerleaders had the right outfits? It all made good sense to Martin.

Now the question was—how to get the $42.50 plus tax

he needed out of the drawer. Martin quickly figured the tax so he would know the exact amount to get. After all, he wasn't a thief. How is he to do it? Certainly it would have to be after lunch. And certainly it wasn't going to be easy. The cashier always took the cash drawer out of the register as soon as lunch was over and carried it back to the cafeteria manager's office. There Martin wasn't sure what happened to it but he was positive it just wasn't left sitting out someplace. The cafeteria manager must have a safe or something. And Martin was no safe-cracker.

In his mind he formed the idea for a new adventure in which he would have to blow up a safe—maybe in the politician's office to get the evidence he needed to show that the politician was taking over Jennie's house for greedy reasons. It would be dangerous and would have to be done quickly. Martin imagined himself placing the dynamite charges. Or should it be nitroglycerine? That was much more dangerous—he'd seen someone use that in a movie. They couldn't shake it up on the way or they'd blow themselves up. Maybe he should . . .

Then he heard the bell ring. It was time for the fifth period. He shook his head as if startled. The bell, however, had brought him back to the task at hand. He had to get some of that money for Jennie's shoes. He walked slowly out of the cafeteria. He had to think of a plan.

All afternoon Martin sat in class paying no attention to what was going on. In his head, however, he was busy devising a scheme. Finally, he had it! He looked around suddenly to see if someone might have been spying on his mind when he hit upon his idea. No one was paying any attention to him.

He cut the final class of the day. He was excited. Besides, he needed to look over the school's ventilation system and then get everything ready.

By the next morning everything was in place. Martin was a bit tired because he was awake most of the night reviewing his plans. By the time he was sure they were right and would work, he was too excited to sleep. However, he was aware he needed to appear as calm as he could in school. He tried to pay attention to his first two classes and contribute something that he felt would make him fit in more—seem more like the other kids.

Then he cut the third period class. He slipped outside the school and found the rags and kerosene he'd hidden in the bushes. Quickly he took them and an old trash can to a huge unlocked storage room in the basement. Once in the room, he placed the barrel under a portion of the ceiling pipes he had figured out yesterday fed directly into the cafeteria's ventilation system. Then he loosened a section of the pipe and let it hang open pointing down toward the barrel.

Martin built a small fire in the metal barrel. He was careful not to place too much material in it so that the flames would reach up and set anything on fire. He had soaked some rags in a solution so that they would smoke a lot. Soon he had a very smoky fire going. It rapidly filled the storage room. Martin could barely keep from choking as he fanned the fire just to make sure it was going well. Lunch would be just about starting and he wanted to make sure the smoke got to the cafeteria before anyone except the cashier and the counter women were there.

Quickly Martin left the storage area, ran upstairs, and pulled the fire alarm in the main hall. As the clanging sounded through the halls, doors quickly opened. Students and teachers began pouring out into the halls and then out of the building.

Martin fled toward the cafeteria. He could see smoke pouring down from the ventilators in the cafeteria ceiling. The counter women and the cashier were still standing there as if they were not sure what to do. It was clear they had not been there when the practice fire drills were conducted (usually fairly early in the morning or late in the afternoon). The hassle of having everyone leave half-eaten lunches sitting on the tables to get cold or warm or soggy or whatever, was a sufficient deterrent to the principal to never have one at lunch.

Martin charged into the cafeteria. "Everyone out," Martin yelled. "It's a bad fire. You may be trapped if you don't get out."

The startled women began to scurry for the doors. Out of the corner of his eye, Martin watched the cashier. She grabbed her purse from underneath the cashier's stand. Then she took the key out of the top of the cash register, locking it so it wouldn't work.

"Damn," thought Martin. "Damn." He had hoped she would forget in the panic.

However, Martin was also prepared in case she did take the key. "Everyone out," he yelled again and charged across the cafeteria toward the exit leading to a hall and the outside. He managed to arrive at the door at the same time as the cashier and bumped into her with such force that she was knocked into the wall. Her purse spilled and the key dropped.

"Oh," said Martin. With lightning speed, he ducked down and scooped up all the purse's contents, and the key, and appeared to throw them back into the purse. He dropped the key down his shirt as he bent over.

"My gosh, I'm sorry," he said, rising and shoving the purse into the dazed cashier's hand. "C'mon, let's get out of here." A quick glance at the smoke curling ever further down from the ceiling and the cashier needed no further urging. Martin followed her all the way to the outside door and then at the last minute darted aside. As the door closed he ran back into the cafeteria.

The smoke was getting thicker, but Martin knew it couldn't last much longer. He hadn't put that much in the barrel. He ran to the cash register and put in the key. He pushed a couple of keys and then hit the button that opened it. The cash drawer slid towards him. There was the change for the day. Martin quickly took what he needed. The exact amount and no more. Then he slammed the drawer shut and put the key down where the cashier usually kept her purse. Sooner or later she'd see it there. Then he ran out of the cafeteria.

Martin found the rest of the afternoon disconcerting. The fire trucks had finally gone, yet things were still terribly unsettled. Classes started late and no one seemed to want to work. Students buzzed with rumors about a trash can in a storeroom and who might have started the false fire and why. In all of his planning of the fire, Martin hadn't considered that the other students and the teachers might be affected, and that classes might be unproductive all afternoon. He hadn't meant to do that and it bothered him. It took the edge off his feeling of success and left him unexpectedly feeling down.

However, by the time Martin got to the shoe store after school his enthusiasm was high again. He waited impatiently for the salesman to get to him.

"I'd like a pair of girls' red and white saddle shoes," he told the man when it became his turn. He remembered to say "girls' " so the man wouldn't tell him again they didn't carry boys'.

"What size?" the man asked, eyeing the number of customers waiting.

"Size?" All of a sudden, Martin realized he didn't have the faintest idea what size Jennie wore.

"What size?" the man repeated.

"She didn't tell me," Martin said lamely, realizing there was no way he could get the shoes if he didn't know the size.

"Well, why don't you have her come in and we'll be glad to fit her," the man said. He started to move away toward the next customer, but looked at Martin as he did in case Martin wanted to add anything.

"That's class," Martin thought. "The shoe men in this store give you the feeling they're helping you even when they aren't. Maybe that's what you pay the extra twenty bucks for."

Martin nodded to the shoe man as a signal he was releasing him to wait on the next customer and then moved disappointedly toward the door. He paused near the door. He could buy a pair of any size shoes and Jennie could bring them in and exchange them for her right size. No, that would ruin everything. Even though the shoe-store man didn't know him, he might describe him to Jennie and she might figure out that he had bought the shoes for her. No, he didn't want to do that.

Martin started the long walk back home. Getting Jennie's shoe size seemed more impossible than getting the money. There was money all over the city that could be gotten if one was clever. However, there was only one shoe size for Jennie's feet.

Martin couldn't believe he had come this far only to fail. His shoulders sagged and he stared at the ground as he went along. He even kicked patches of grass growing in the sidewalk. Oh hell. He couldn't ask any of Jennie's friends to help because they were not his friends. And besides, he couldn't let anyone else know because, well, because this was a private thing. He was the one to rescue Jennie and letting someone else in would take away the credit.

No, he had to do it by himself. "Oh," Jennie's voice echoed once again in his ears. "Oh, what am I going to do? What am I going to do?" Martin also began to feel remorseful. He didn't think of using the school's money to buy Jennie's shoes as stealing but certainly his having the money without buying her shoes put a different light on things. He didn't want the money. He didn't want to be a thief.

Martin walked along. How to find out her size? . . . Suddenly he had it. It wasn't just her feet that would tell the size. Her current saddle shoes would also show what her size was. But when would she take her shoes off so he could find out the size? One time would be when she went to bed. Martin tried to imagine creeping in through her bedroom window. Would it be on the first or second floor? Martin had never been inside her house so he didn't know. Make it the first floor, that would be easier. He imagined crawling in through Jennie's window after it got dark.

He moved stealthily to her bedside. She was sleeping. He reached down for a shoe. She stirred and opened her eyes.

Martin then shifted his dream. In his fantasy, he couldn't just say to her, "I need your shoe size."

Martin put his hand over her mouth so she wouldn't scream, and motioned for her to be quiet. Then he signaled her to follow him. He helped her out of the window. Her beautiful body, curved and soft, felt heavenly through her flimsy pink gown. Together they crept to the garage where Martin glanced nervously around. When he was sure they were not being observed, he led her inside, lit his flashlight and showed her the documents from the politician's safe.

"You see," he explained, "this is why he is condemning your house and making you move—because of the plans for the new expressway."

Jennie gasped in surprise. "I've got to tell my parents," she said.

"No," Martin told her. "This man will stop at nothing. If he thinks your parents know the real reason, he might try to dispose of them." He said the last slowly so that Jennie got the clear meaning. "I even hate to involve you," Martin said, "however, I need your help. Here's my plan to save your home and get rid of that politician once and for all." Martin quickly began to outline . . .

HONK! A loud horn startled Martin so much that he jumped. He looked up to see that he had started across the street before the light had changed. He jumped back on the curb. That brought him back to reality and the problem of getting Jennie's shoe size.

What other times does she take her shoes off, he thought. Then he remembered Wednesday was the day tenth-grade girls went swimming. She had to take her shoes off to go swimming.

A week later Martin woke up smiling for the third straight day. He reached down under his bed and pulled out a box. The outside read "Saddle. Style #498, Size 6, Red and White $42.50." It was the box for Jennie's shoes.

Martin recalled creeping around the girls' locker room to find Jennie's clothes and underneath them her shoes and, of course, her shoe size. Boy, if he had been caught handling her clothes, he never would have lived that down. But he hadn't been caught, and it really hadn't been that hard getting her shoe size. It had almost been harder putting the new shoes in Jennie's homeroom desk without being seen.

Martin wished he could have been there when she found them. But it would have been too obvious since he wasn't in her homeroom. Actually, it was enough to have watched her from the stands as she danced in front of the crowd in her red and white shoes. She was so pretty and so happy. Did she wonder who had done it for her? Was she dreaming of the hero who was able to make her dreams come true, bring her happiness?

Martin imagined himself standing humbly in front of her. No, wait a minute, he wasn't alone. Peter Dunkin stood there too.

Jennie was looking confused as if trying to choose between them. Peter was laying claim to all kinds of things. Martin didn't say anything. Just slowly, from behind his back, he brought forth the shoe box.

Jennie stared in astonishment as she saw the box. "Then it was you!" she gasped. "It was you all along!"

Peter was trying to say something but Jennie didn't even hear him. She looked straight at Martin. "Oh, Martin! It was you all along!" And her gaze was filled with love and adoration.

"Yes," said Martin, "but 'til now, I didn't want you to know!" And with that he swept her into his arms.

The noise of his father gargling in the bathroom brought Martin back to reality. He glanced down at the shoe box in his hands. Jennie's shoes had been in that box. He would cherish it forever.

LYDIA

Lydia swam lazily in the warm water at the beach. She had worn her bathing suit under her regular clothes because she had not been sure she would find a place to change. Her flowered bathing suit seemed strangely out of place in the clear water. She saw no fish or other forms of life but here and there dark patches of rock and coral rose up into view from the bottom. Since she wasn't sure what sea creatures might live in such underwater formations, she swam around and not over them, and touched her feet down only where she could see plain sand.

When Lydia finally came out of the water, she found the beach sand too sticky to lie on, so she picked up her slacks, top, and hat, and carried them over to one of the huge rocks that lay near the beach. She boosted herself on the rock to dry off.

Lydia looked around. Underneath one of the scraggly trees in the grassy area she noticed a wood and metal picnic table had been placed. It was another one of those oddities. Here in all this primitive land, there was a modern picnic table. She turned back to the water and sat staring out. Somewhere in another part of the world was her family, her home. They seemed familiar yet unreal to her, just as this place now seemed strange but real.

Lydia sat thinking a long time. Finally, it was the lowered angle of the sun's rays that caught her attention. She looked around. Everyone else had gone but she hadn't seen them go. With a start she glanced at her watch and realized she should have started back at least an hour before. Nevertheless, she hesitated. Remembrance of the loneliness and pain awaiting her in the empty villa welled up. She bent over and ran her hand down the side of the rock. The sadness was always inside her. But for a little while today, she had walked away from some of the pain. She tried to store up the moments now surrounding her.

The sun continued to sink and finally Lydia rose to begin the walk back. How far had she come on this road? Off in the vague distance she saw a part of the jutting coastline that might or might not be the town. She knew that in walking back she would be faced with the endless curves, cutting off, curving in and out, opening up, and the road slanting up and down, turning, ever turning.

There was no sea breeze now. The afternoon rays beat harshly down on the road. The small rocks in the road seemed bigger than when Lydia had walked over them the first time. She began to look for patches of plain dirt to step on as her feet began to hurt from the rough surface.

Another curve, another bend. Lydia felt the heat on her skin. The sun screen lotion she had put on before she left in the morning had washed off in the water. Lydia was also aware that more of her concentration was going into the walking—

where her feet went, her leg motion. She was beginning to get thirsty again. The thermos of water she had brought from her aunt's house had been finished earlier at the beach and now hung empty and useless from her waist.

Lydia strained to catch sight of something familiar to tell her how far she had to go. But traveling in reverse made every curve and hillside seem new to her. It was as if she had never come this way at all. Fleetingly, she wondered if it wouldn't be the same when her despair and hurt started to go away—whether the way back from anguish and despair would be as unfamiliar as the way in.

She twisted her ankle on a stone she hadn't noticed in the road. There was a momentary smarting that then went away. She had to be more careful about where she was going.

An hour passed and then more time. Finally she saw the inlet where the hotel was being built. The chinking noise had stopped. Almost all of the workers had already gone home for the day. Only a few were putting tools away at the base of the structure. Although she was grateful for the silence as she passed, she felt worried. It was later than she wanted it to be. She struggled up the road leading out of the inlet and around the next curve. There was a long way still to go. If only the truck with the little boy and his father would come by, she would accept a ride this time.

The afternoon haze spread lower over the rocks. Lydia looked down at the ocean. The water beneath her noisily splashed up and fell back, splashed up and fell back, like dogs leaping and baying at a treed animal. Lydia hurried on. Her feet often fell sideways off the varied shaped rocks in the road; her ankles strained with each step. She tugged unconsciously at her sleeves trying to get them down further on her arms. She was aware the sun was baking the exposed parts of her body—arms, wrists, hands, feet. She even felt the heat through her hat and the clothes on her back and wondered if they were giving her much protection at all. At least her bathing suit made an extra layer of cloth over some of her skin. She pushed herself to go on. There was now a pulsating sense in her body. She was thirsty. The hills were endless. The road led continually to a curve only to reveal another lonely curve to be conquered ahead.

Another half hour, another climbing up and down of the road. Lydia knew she was going slower. She no longer heard the birds in the sky or the roar of the water. She was fully inside herself now, moving only her body. Desolate feelings began to well up inside—the loneliness of why she was there, all alone, struggling on the road. Still more curves. Another hour passed. Finally, she staggered to a halt. She longed for a rock to sit on, but there was none so she just sank down to the ground. For the first time the thought occurred to her she might not make it back. She didn't want that—not here.

Lydia took a couple of deep breaths and struggled to her feet. She was surprised at the pain in her ankles. She forced her legs forward and tried to get her stride. But her feet kept sliding awkwardly off the small rocks in the dirt road. Her ankles were weakened. She gritted her teeth. She must concentrate. She must watch her steps even more—try to step in the dirt, not on the stones. Each step had to be thought out, planned, maneuvered. The pain in the calves of her legs joined the pain in her ankles. Her body was tense and ached from the concentration.

Lydia staggered on. Her mind began to hurt. Another hour passed. Then two. Lydia felt helpless. She felt alone. And she was alone, she knew. Why? Why? Why? She wondered. Why did it have to happen? The pain in her mind, heart, and body seemed to fuse. Such enormous pain, the pain she had felt for months, the pain she could not numb, the pain that was greater than physical pain, rose up and joined with the physical pain. Why? Why? Why? Over and over in the blur of pain she asked Why? Then she felt the final burning inside her. The pain had come together and now the final destruction was taking place. There would be nothing left inside her but a desert—just barrenness.

Lydia stumbled on. Somewhere in the back of her mind she was aware of her life as it had been—shaded streets, city sidewalks, buses, fluttery curtains and a white bedroom set, the face of her school principal, department stores. And she saw superimposed on it the isolation of the coastline, the tans and browns, the searing heat, the strange faces of the people in the town. Then all the images faded. Her mouth was dry and she felt all her concentration drawn to her body's need for water. She looked around helplessly. She needed water. But there was no water between her and the town somewhere up ahead. She thought with bitter irony of the endless salt water down the side of the cliffs. She went on for another half hour.

Finally up ahead she saw the deserted shacks on the hill. She knew there would be no water there. Except for the villas, houses did not have running water in this land. Yet it meant she was getting closer to the town. She forced her body to keep moving.

Suddenly a large black dog, teeth bared, rushed down the hillside at her. Lydia felt her terror rising. She didn't have the ability to run. She was weak. She kept on watching. The dog charged toward her. Lydia looked desperately for someone to emerge from one of the gray shacks and call the dog. But no one appeared. Surely someone could hear him, and would yell at the dog, or run to get him. But no one appeared. Lydia turned to wave her arms at the dog. She didn't know what to do. Should she turn her back and try to go on? Should she stay facing him? The dog stopped. "I've got to get away from here," she thought. She turned and tried to go on down the road, glancing back. The dog followed her and made several menacing lunges. How long would he follow her?

Would he not return to his home? If he launched a final attack, he would overwhelm her, she was sure.

Lydia's heart was beating wildly. She looked for a stick to defend herself but there were only rocks and dirt here as elsewhere. There were no bushes to break a branch off from, even if she had had the strength. She felt her panic increase. The dog was closer now. His black eyes in his massive black head sparkled hate.

Then the dog hesitated in the road. Perhaps, she thought, he's stopped. But then he made a major rush at her. Oh no, she thought. Then as she stood there yelling and waving her arms, miraculously he stopped within a few feet of her. Was it being kicked at in his daily life, or some motion she had made unwittingly, that signaled even a helpless girl had power over him? Or had Lydia unknowingly reached the magic limits of his territory? She didn't know. But with angry growls the dog turned and retreated.

Quickly Lydia turned and started to move on. The dog stood barking. All her courage spent, her body racked with pain, Lydia pushed on. Somewhere up ahead, across town, was her aunt's villa, water, a bed. She strained every muscle. The forbidding stone walls of the three elegant villas on this side of town loomed up. Their gates were closed—no life this time of the year. On the way out of town, the lavish deserted villas had looked enticing. Now they seemed desolate and lonely. Lydia slowly forced her legs to work, painfully carrying her past them step by step. Her body was bent over. She was stumbling forward.

The road made a sharp descent. Then Lydia came to the town and the street she wanted. She turned down it and made another turn. The Dairy Queen stood just ahead. Because of dusk, it already had its yellow light bulbs on. Its incongruity seemed all the more strange to her now. It was like an oasis in the middle of nowhere. Tears welled up. It was a bit of civilization, a bit of home.

Several townspeople and two off-season tourists sat at the tables under their orange and white umbrellas. Lydia staggered to the order window. "Two large lemonades," her voice came out in a whisper. She counted out her money and looked for a place to sit. The only table available was one without an umbrella. The final rays of the sun beat down on her reddened wrists and hands as she tore at the papers covering the straws. She shoved them frantically through the plastic covers on the cups. She drank gulps at first and then took long sips. As she drank, her overall pain began to individualize itself. She felt the searing sunburn on her arms and feet, the throbbing pain in her ankles and legs, the aches in her body, the rawness of her sunburned hands.

Lydia finished the second lemonade and then rose slowly. To her surprise, she learned that stopping had intensified the physical pain. In agony, she moved off toward her aunt's villa. Once safely inside, she wanted to sink down by the door. "But," she thought, "if I lie down now, I'll never get up. I've got to take care of myself."

Lydia moved to the bath area and stood there weakly, fumbling to get her clothes off. Her bathing suit was the hardest. It almost took more strength than she had and was agonizingly painful when it rubbed her body. Breathing irregularly, she reached over to the sink and soaked a washcloth. She patted her face with cool water. She found a tube of sunburn cream in her bag. She went into the bedroom and sat on the edge of the bed. Chills began running up and down her body. She slowly applied the soothing cream on her sunburn.

Then painful as it was, she lay down and covered herself with a bedspread. Once she had adjusted it, she tried to move as little as possible so it wouldn't touch her sunburn. She shivered.

Then despite the agonizing pain, the aches, the tiredness, the chills, the world began to disappear. She fell into a deep sleep, one of the deepest in her life. A sleep so deep that no dreams, no thoughts, no awareness of any kind could enter. Unknowingly, Lydia had finally found the oblivion she wanted. For eighteen hours she lay, as if in the deepest nonexistence, almost what death must be like. But Lydia was alive, and inside her body began again its work of repairing a human being, torn and tortured.

GEORGE

George could not believe what was going on. First his sister Geraldine had done a dumb thing like tipping over another girl's sewing machine at school because she thought the girl had purposely torn the blouse Geraldine was making. The machine broke when it hit the floor and that meant destroying school property. The police had been called. The principal decided not to press charges but insisted a policeman take Geraldine home and give a warning to George's parents about Geraldine's behavior.

And then, of course, a fluke. Boooom! The minute the policeman had gotten inside their house, he'd smelled the pot George was smoking. Jeez, those guys had good noses. George's mother and father had never smelled it all the times he'd used it. But then, of course, George had been careful to open a window and would try to blow a fan around before he ever opened his bedroom door.

Anyway, just because of dumb Geraldine, he'd gotten busted over the weed. He'd had to go to juvenile court and ended up being put on probation, and his dad had grounded him for the rest of the school year. What a bummer. Anyway, thank God he hadn't had a big stash but just what was rolled in his hand. He might have been sent to a correctional place. His mother had treated the whole thing like it almost never happened. Maybe it was because of her concern over Geraldine. George didn't know. But for his father it had happened. In the first two weeks his father came down on him so hard, he really thought he would just run away. But, of course, he knew if he violated his probation, there would be a law officer after him, not just his dad.

But then Geraldine had really gone off the deep end and stolen some camping equipment from the sporting-goods store at the shopping mall. She said that her teacher made her do it as part of a social-studies experiment about survival. Only trouble was Geraldine got caught and they weren't studying survival in her social studies class. Stupid Geraldine.

So George's parents were back in court again with their other child and this made George's father even more outraged. His mother treated it as if it were no big deal—after all, Geraldine had returned the things and admitted she hadn't done it for school. As a matter of fact, she didn't know why she did it. That seemed to satisfy his mother.

But it didn't satisfy the judge, who insisted that Geraldine be sent to a psychiatrist. Actually, George thought that was a good idea. He never did understand Geraldine. At the same time, he hated the idea that someone in their family needed psychiatric help. It was as if the whole family were mentally diseased because Geraldine needed a shrink. He waited hopefully for signs the psychiatrist was helping Geraldine. But after a month Geraldine was as moody and weird as ever.

A psychiatrist is a medical doctor (M.D.) who has been trained to evaluate mental-health problems and to treat them with psychological methods, physical therapy, and drugs. Usually, psychiatrists have had four years of undergraduate college, three to four years of medical school, a hospital internship of one year, and a three-year psychiatric residency. Psychiatrists who become psychoanalysts have even further training.

The psychiatrist at one point suggested that the whole family come in for what he called family therapy. But George's dad wouldn't go and he wouldn't let George or his mother go either (not that George wanted to). His dad said it wasn't them who were nuts; it was Geraldine for all the stupid stunts she had been pulling lately. George laughed at that. What the hell did he care.

Mental-health problems used to be called "mental illness." There are no firm rules as to whether certain feelings or behaviors are mental-health problems. In war, for example, people do things that in peacetime would be considered insane. Therefore, circumstances and the individuals involved often contribute to definitions about what is a mental-health problem. Nevertheless, most people do not like to be thought of as having mental problems. This then becomes one of the biggest obstacles to recognizing the need for help and getting it. Seeking help is a mature way to deal with problems. Yet not all adults recognize this, and therefore even parents may have difficulty helping young people overcome their attitudes about needing and using mental-health services.

Things at home were really sour. Everyone was uptight. George heard his dad and mom talking late into the nights and he could sense a real strain in their relationship. He could imagine his mother wondering what they did wrong and his father pushing that aside. He knew his father thought if everyone tried to be more like him, they'd be better people.

At first his father seemed to treat Geraldine differently. Every time Geraldine picked on George and he snapped back, his dad jumped on him. At seventy-five dollars an hour, George figured his dad didn't want anyone messing up Geraldine more so she'd have to spend a longer time seeing the psychiatrist. George happened to know his dad's insurance reimbursed him for half of the psychiatrist's fee. But his dad preferred to ignore that, and constantly complained about what he felt was the psychiatrist's outrageous charge.

George was so fed up he didn't know what to do. What a lousy break to be born into his family, have weird old Geraldine as a sister, and his mom and dad as parents.

Then things suddenly changed. George's dad conveyed to George that he wanted him to be "normal." For George's father, normal boys had friends, normal boys dated, got good grades, normal boys played sports. Normal boys did not hang out in their rooms and read books.

So suddenly George found himself no longer grounded but was instead being sent out of the house constantly. "Why don't you . . ." came the suggestions. George again felt he was being controlled, directed, squeezed through a mold. But at least he was not being grounded. At least he could get out. As a matter of fact, at this moment George sat in his room contemplating where he would go after dinner. He certainly didn't want to stay home.

"George, dear," his mother called to him from down the hall. She could never just come to his room and talk to him. She had to start talking the minute she hit the hall. "What do you want for dinner tonight? I've got some of that chicken and noodle casserole we had Thursday or I could make stuffed pork chops."

"Oh, God, here we go again," George thought. "Doesn't she understand I don't give a damn what we have for dinner? Dinner is the last thing I care about. I just want to be left alone."

George's mother entered the room. "Did you hear me? I was wondering what you wanted for dinner tonight."

George wanted to reply, "Shit, mother, just do your own thing, huh. Who gives a damn!" Instead he replied, "Whatever you think the rest of the family would like."

"Dear, that's so thoughtful of you." His mother walked over and gave him a hug.

George pulled away but his mother didn't seem to notice. "I know you are worried about Geraldine, George, just as we are, but I really don't want that to affect your life."

So now his mother was picking up that normal stuff just like his father. George grimaced. He didn't give a shit about Geraldine. He just wished she weren't his sister, weren't in his life.

"But everything's going to work out all right, I'm sure. Geraldine just needs some time to adjust to growing up."

There she was, his mom with her damn naive attitude. George knew Geraldine wasn't going to be all right. That she really was messed up. He didn't know when or how it had happened but Geraldine was messed up and there was no quick miraculous cure even at seventy-five dollars an hour.

"Oh, dear," his mother said, "I was thinking about Geraldine and I forgot what you said—chicken and noodles or stuffed pork chops?"

George couldn't stand it any longer. He lifted up his arm and smelled under it. "Oh, my God, I've got a subcutaneous bacteria creating a malodorous nauseating condition in my armpit area." He jumped up. "My God, this can't go on. H_2O must be applied immediately." He danced wildly out of the room, ran down the hall, turned on the shower and without even adjusting the temperature, jumped in with his clothes on.

"George, what? . . . " His mother's voice faded as he turned up the water. He leaned against the shower stall. What had made him do a crazy thing like this? Maybe he was going crazy. Maybe he was going bananas like Geraldine. Jeez, though, he just couldn't stand his mother asking so politely for him to decide the world: "What do you want for breakfast?" "Is it cold out—which coat do you think I need to wear?" "Where do you think I ought to set this bouquet of flowers?" "Do you think we ought to ask your grandmother here for dinner on Mother's Day or take her out to eat?" And it didn't seem to matter what it was or who it was—she always asked whoever was closest so you couldn't even think that she particularly trusted your opinion. She just asked whoever was around. She never just went ahead and did something.

Why, one day George had even heard her asking the mailman where he thought she ought to put her new holly bushes. When later George told her he thought it was stupid to ask the mailman about planting bushes in their yard, she had replied that she thought since he saw so many yards in his work, he might have a good idea where they would look best.

George sighed unhappily. There was his mom, forever optimistic, forever cheerful, but never deciding anything. And there was his dad, forever acting harassed and pushy, telling everyone what to do all the time. And there was Geraldine all messed up, deciding all the wrong things. Where did that leave him?

George felt sad for a minute. Life could be so painful, so miserable. He couldn't wait till he could get out on his own away from his family. Surely there was more to life than this. Maybe he would join the army rather than go to college. That would get him far, far away. He'd have his own paycheck; it wouldn't be much, but since the army would pay for his room and board, whatever it paid him in salary would be his.

George slowly turned off the shower. His shirt was dripping, his pants were dripping. His clothes gave him a cold, soggy, miserable feeling. But until he could finish school, he was stuck here with these weirdos. The only thing to do was to blot everything out as much as possible. Try to get by with as little interaction as possible. School was almost over for the year. In another week George would turn seventeen, and a long time ago his dad had promised when he turned seventeen, he could get a driver's license and start using the car.

George hadn't raised the subject with his dad because of all that was going on. Maybe he would still let him. Although the fact that he'd screwed up the lawn and had used marijuana was still fresh in his dad's mind, so was his dad's desire for George to be normal. And if George could show him how "normal" boys were driving . . ."

George dripped back to his room, leaving water stains on the hall floor. His mother was nowhere in sight. He took off his clothes, and not wanting to get his floor any wetter and not wanting to go back to the bathroom for fear of meeting his mom, he dropped his clothes out the bedroom window. Only after he had let them fall did he realize his mother had planted snapdragons and zinnias along that side of the house. The tender plants were immediately crushed under the weight of his sodden clothes.

"Oh, hell." Well, he'd get the clothes later before anyone saw what had ruined the plants. He'd probably have to break off a few more plants elsewhere too, just so it wouldn't be so obvious that the plants under his window were the only broken ones. What a hassle.

George dressed in a bad mood. He couldn't decide whether he was angry at himself for not having thrown his clothes out further onto the grass or because he was just fed up with everything.

The phone rang. George debated about answering it. If it was for him, he would much prefer getting the call himself. It was that the call was contaminated if it had to come through any member of his family. On the other hand, if it was not for him, it probably was for Geraldine or his mom. The last thing he wanted to do was to explain to one of Geraldine's weirdo girlfriends that she had gone to see her psychiatrist after school that day and wouldn't be home for another half hour or so. Even worse than that was the thought it might be for his mom, and that he would have to go find her and face her. It was bad enough having pulled the armpit scene and rushed out on her for the shower. Now he was guilty of breaking her plants too. George decided to let the phone ring.

The phone rang about four times and then stopped ringing. George assumed his mother had picked it up. He lay down on his bed. He just didn't feel like doing anything. He felt bitter about his relationship with his parents. The other kids complained about their parents, too, but their hate and resentment didn't seem at all like his. He had tried to talk to Brodie about it once or twice. Brodie had listened like a good friend, but he could tell Brodie didn't really know what he was talking about. Brodie's mom and dad were nice enough sorts who laughed a lot. Although Brodie felt hassled at times, too, he never had the blowups with his family like George had with his parents.

George had not lain down long when his mother opened the door to his room without knocking and came in. George sat up angrily and was about to say something when he stopped. The look on his mother's face was unlike any he had ever seen her have. George sat still trying to imagine what had happened.

"The psychiatrist called. He's just put Geraldine in the psychiatric ward at the hospital. He said it's for her own protection. She's had a breakdown, he said." His mother looked at him pleadingly as if she wanted him to make sense out of it for her.

George didn't know what it all meant but he knew Geraldine must be very ill. Nevertheless, he felt stunned by the news. Even more, he continued to be struck by his mother's expression. Behind her pleading was a look of awareness. Something had finally gotten through to her. She had finally realized it wasn't just all a game with Geraldine. It wasn't just all a little adventure that would pass quickly. Geraldine was sick, really sick.

Most kinds of mental illness are categorized into two basic types: neurosis and psychosis. Neuroses are sometimes referred to as emotional rather than mental illnesses. People who are suffering from a neurosis are unreasonably anxious about something in their life, even though they are in touch with reality. For example, they may have a phobia or an unreasonable fear of something. They may experience hypochondria, in which they believe they are ill or about to become ill even when they are physically healthy.

Depression is another neurosis that goes beyond the down-in-the-dumps feeling most people occasionally experience. Depressed persons may experience physical symptoms such as backaches, headaches, an inability to sleep, and exhaustion. They may feel desperately unhappy. Mild depressions can grow into a kind of despondency that drives people to suicide.

Another form of neurosis is the anxiety reaction in which people who have it constantly fear something terrible will happen to them although they have little or no idea what that might be. Psychosomatic illnesses are real illnesses that seem to be caused by psychological conflicts.

Psychoses are mental illnesses of a very serious nature. Organic psychoses are produced by physical causes. Functional psychoses do not as yet have clearly defined, known causes.

Organic psychosis can occur due to a head injury or when the body experiences a negative reaction to alcohol, drugs, and certain poisons. Syphilis of the brain is a form of organic psychosis as are two diseases of old age: one in which the arteries harden and hamper the functions of the brain, and another in which the brain cells deteriorate and eventually wear out.

Functional psychoses are either diseases that interfere with a person's thinking or are diseases of mood or feeling. Diseases *that interfere with a person's thinking are often referred to as schizophrenia. People who have schizophrenia may be unable to think about the simplest problems; they may be silly or confused in their behavior and talk. Sometimes the person may sound and act quite reasonable, but the things that bother her or him are completely imaginary. People who have this problem may be excessively jealous, and have beliefs that they are great or famous or very special. Some withdraw from the world and stand motionless for hours.*

Diseases of mood or feeling are often referred to as affective disorders or as manic-depressive psychosis. Often, a person with this kind of problem is either extremely happy or extremely depressed.

Some people who are not neurotic or psychotic are called mentally disturbed because they have personality disorders. For example, they may express violent and uncontrollable rage. Some may be irresponsible or may commit crimes and have no regret. Others constantly try to draw attention to themselves.

Among other problems many mental-health professionals consider mental disorders are alcoholism and drug dependence. People who use drugs and drinking to escape from the unhappiness they experience in the real world are often people who are not capable of solving their problems, and who are anxious and frustrated. Drug-taking and drinking do not solve any problems and indeed eventually can become problems in and of themselves. They can lead to illness and death.

There are also many people who have relatively minor problems, but the problems interfere with their ability to live up to their potential or relate to others in the way they would like.

———————

George wanted to be charitable. He had a half impulse to go put his arms around his mother, comfort her, tell her it would be all right. But his other impulse was to savor the recognition that at long last she was tuned into something. He didn't want to be the cause of her slipping back into her nice everything-will-be-all-right naive world. So he just sat there looking at her, watching her becoming aware and frightened.

Finally his mother had struggled with her feelings enough to let something else come out. "What," she began in a anguished voice. "What will your father say?"

"Oh, God." George had forgotten about his father. "Oh, God. What would he say? What would he do? George longed for some marijuana—anything to get him through the explosion that was bound to come. Oh God, what a mess. God, he needed a smoke.

The poor mental health of a parent or a sibling can affect other children in the family. All family members including children have a right to have their questions about the person who is having a problem answered as simply and directly as possible. Living with someone with poor mental health is stressful. Many children of parents who are either physically or mentally ill may show some maladjustment. However, studies show that the majority of children of parents suffering from major mental illnesses do not themselves become mentally ill. If ways can be found to allow children to feel they are helping either the parent or the sibling who has mental-health problems, it would be desirable. Parents of adolescents or children with mental-health problems may want to seek support for the stress they experience from professionals or other parents in similar situations.

5

Can Anyone Hear Me? Does Anyone Care?

MARTIN

Because Jennie wore the shoes Martin had gotten for her, Martin felt closer to her than ever. He was, therefore, even more eager to spend time on his dreams. They almost always included Jennie.

Sometimes Martin was amazed that so many good stories could come out of his head. His adventures were wildly varied. In some he had fine cars or a motorbike; once he even had a speedboat. Sometimes he was struggling and poor; at other times he had endless money in his pocket. Most of all, though, he was clever and athletic and able to solve fantastic problems and do amazing feats. Whenever Jennie was in his stories, she grew to admire him and love him.

Of course, Martin knew that in school Jennie didn't notice him, but that was, he felt, because she didn't know the real him. Occasionally when he saw her, he got ready to approach her just as if he was the person in his fantasies. Somehow, though, he always remembered before he got to her that his fantasies weren't quite real. Then they would pass each other in silence without her appearing to be aware he even existed.

Fantasies can actually be helpful to adolescents. However, if they are never altered by the adolescent's awareness of reality, they can become destructive to the adolescent's mental health.

This day, however, Martin felt agitated about being unable to talk to Jennie. He had seen her crying right after first period. She was actually standing in the hall outside a classroom crying. Several kids were clustered around her. Martin walked up and stood with them, trying to understand what was going on. "What happened?" he asked the person next to him. She shrugged and said she didn't know. The bell for the next class rang. One of the girls put her arm around Jennie's shoulder and led her into the girls' bathroom. Martin wanted to hang around until they came out, on the chance he could overhear their conversation and find out what had happened. But all the kids were disappearing into classrooms. He would be the only one in the hall. That would look funny.

He toyed with the idea of waiting outside her next class and just asking what was wrong, but he wasn't sure he'd have the courage to do that. Maybe it was something she wouldn't want him to know.

Martin moped through his next two classes and felt very distracted at lunch. He had never seen Jennie cry before. Even so, this wasn't just a regular cry, he thought. She really had been crying hard.

After lunch when he again saw Jennie, she was sitting outside with three of the other cheerleaders. She was crying again. Obviously she had been so upset she had skipped lunch—and upset enough that three of her friends had skipped lunch with her. Martin stared out the window at the foursome for a long time. He couldn't hear what they were saying through the glass, but their distress, particularly Jennie's, was obvious. Martin had to find out what was going on.

He started questioning everyone who might know. Finally he found out. Cheerleaders had to get grades of C or above, or they couldn't be cheerleaders, and Jennie had just been told by her Spanish teacher that she was going to get a D. That would mean she couldn't be a cheerleader next semester. No wonder she was upset!

Martin's eyes narrowed in anger. He had always thought Miss Battaglia was a scrooge. Now he knew it. The old bat. What did Spanish matter anyway? It wasn't something you were ever going to use unless you were Puerto Rican or Cuban or Mexican, in which case you knew it anyway. Couldn't that old witch tell that Jennie was the prettiest and the best of the cheerleaders? What would it hurt to just give Jennie the C even if she had done D work?

The more he thought about it, the madder Martin got. Miss Battaglia had hurt Jennie and hurt her badly. She had to pay. Martin tightened his jaw. Miss Battaglia had to pay.

That night Martin began his attack. First he made several telephone calls to Miss Battaglia's home. Every time she answered he made a low weird sound. Then he refused to make any other sounds although she kept asking "Who is this?" After she hung up, he'd wait a bit and then call again. He kept it up until late into the night when finally she didn't answer. Twice in the middle of the night he called and just let her phone ring anyway.

Martin was up early the next morning. It was raining. And it was garbage collection day so everyone had put the trash cans out by the street. Martin sorted through several trash cans until he had collected a half dozen jars and bottles. He took these to a vacant lot and smashed them. He then carefully put the splinters and pieces into an old pail.

Fortunately the rain was keeping the day dark even later than usual. He hurried to school and located the parking space with Miss Battaglia's name on it. As he scattered the pieces of glass he was careful to make sure they didn't get in anyone else's space. Then he returned home, changed out of his wet clothes, and went to school at the regular time. If his luck held and the rain kept up, she wouldn't notice the pieces of glass until she had driven over them.

When Martin arrived at school he made a point of going to an upstairs hall window before going to his homeroom. He was satisfied to see that the teacher had obviously driven in without seeing the glass and two of her tires were already quite flat. "Two," he thought with satisfaction. That was even better than he had hoped for.

Martin called Miss Battaglia again that evening. The next day he left school early and stopped by the apartment building where Miss Battaglia lived. He couldn't get in any further than the entry hall. But he figured on that, so it was all right. He looked for her mailbox—sure enough he could see mail in it. Carefully, he poured honey into the slot until he saw it run out the bottom and start to drip on the floor. Then he propped the door to the entry hall open. With satisfaction he noticed even before he left that several yellow-jacket bees had flown in and were buzzing around the hallway. By the time Miss Battaglia got home, there would be bees and who knew what else to greet her.

Martin called her again that evening. By the way she answered the phone he could tell she was rattled. However, although it gave him a great deal of satisfaction to know he was getting to her, he had one worry. Jennie was still terribly sad and his making Miss Battaglia "pay" wasn't making Jennie happier.

Suddenly he had an idea. What if Jennie got a perfect grade on her final exam? Then there was no way she could get a D. It would have to be at least a C!

Martin now began to think in earnest. Somehow he had to get a copy of the final Spanish examination. Then he had to find someone who could fill it in perfectly and then he had to put Jennie's name on it and find a way to slip it in with the tests after the kids took them and take hers out! At first it seemed like an overwhelming task to him. Then he remembered that he'd been able to slip a revised form in the politician's portfolio when the man had been trying to get Jennie's house condemned. The politician had then handed the judge the papers that incriminated him rather than proved the house should be condemned. Once again, Martin was lost in half-dream/half-reality—his imagination feeding his idea bank and giving him courage to face his impossible task.

Martin had only one week before the final exam, so he had to work fast. He tried some Spanish-speaking people he knew—suggesting they help him with a special secret project. Everyone refused except one kid who went to college. He immediately figured out Martin wanted help cheating on a test. He was willing to do it, but it fell through when he learned the test was on the Friday he had intended to go to a stock-car race in the next state.

Finally Martin figured out a simpler way to do it—a way he could do it all by himself without involving anyone else. It was a gamble but the odds looked better than most to Martin.

Luiz Bandura was taking Spanish. Luiz was Spanish-speaking already so he really didn't need to take the subject. However, Luiz was not such a terrific student, but since he was on the football team, he had to keep up his grade average. So by taking Spanish, he was assured of at least one good mark. Martin knew Luiz was probably good for a B on the test, and if he had his head together that day he might even get an A. He'd been known to do that before. If Martin could get hold of Luiz's test and change Jennie's answers to match his, then the worst that could happen was that Luiz and Jennie would both get Bs. But if Luiz got an A, then Jennie would have the A she needed to keep on being a cheerleader.

Martin hated gambling on Luiz to get an A. He would have liked a sure thing. But he figured that using Luiz was his best shot. Now all he had to do was figure out how to get Luiz's and Jennie's tests, change Jennie's answers, and then put the tests back before anyone found out they were missing. That was going to be harder.

On Friday, the day of the test, Martin hung around outside Miss Battaglia's door as the kids filed out after the test. He was interested in just two faces—Jennie's and Luiz's. As he had expected, Jennie looked distressed. However, Luiz looked happy. That, at any rate, was a good sign.

If Martin had been sure Miss Battaglia would leave the ungraded tests at school over the weekend, it would have been a lot easier. But Miss Battaglia was an old bat. Since she wasn't married, she probably just sat around and graded tests on weekends. Hence Martin had to act before the end of the school day. If only his plan would work.

Just before the next class ended, Martin walked into Miss Battaglia's room with a pink telephone slip from the principal's office. The message read: "Miss Battaglia, Please call Captain Boxall at the police station between your 6th and 7th period class." Miss Battaglia frowned. She finished collecting the tests from that class and, after putting them in a folder on her desk, left the room. The bell rang, signaling time to change classes.

Martin quickly grabbed the stack of folders from her desk. He sorted through them and found the one marked "5th period"—Jennie's class. One or two of the kids looked strangely at him. "She wants this in the office for some reason," Martin said and hurried out the door. Since Martin didn't take Spanish, the kids would certainly never think he was doing anything illegal. Plus, of course, they would have no idea what folder he had picked up.

Martin hurried down to the boys' gym and sneaked back in a corner behind the lockers. He had just one period in which to pull this off. Quickly he went through the papers had found Jennie's and Luiz's. It was a two-page test. Martin found it was a much more difficult job to change the answers than he imagined. First of all, Luiz's handwriting was not that good. Moreover, Martin's handwriting didn't look like Jennie's. Worst of all, Martin had never had Spanish and since none of it made any sense to him he had to copy it letter by letter.

"Oh, Jennie," Martin murmured several times as he saw how different her test answers were from Luiz's. He erased and changed her answers as rapidly as he could. He didn't know how much time had passed but it seemed as if he surely could not finish in a period. Then he got to a section where Jennie seemed to have it all right. He was grateful to her for helping him out. Finally he finished. He looked at Jennie's two pages of answers. It didn't look great but it was readable. He quickly mixed the two tests back in the folder, making sure they were far apart from each other.

Martin sped back to wait outside Miss Battaglia's class. When the final bell rang, he wandered into Miss Battaglia's class as casually as he could, carefully hiding the folder underneath the books and notebook he was carrying. He hated to go back into her room but he had no choice.

Miss Battaglia saw him approaching her and said, "Who in the office gave you that message?"

Martin said, "No one, I was just passing by your room and I saw it on the hall floor outside so I picked it up and brought it in to you."

"Oh," said Miss Battaglia thoughtfully. "I wonder . . ."

"Why? Is something wrong?" Martin asked, resting his books carefully at the corner of her desk.

"Well, no one seemed to know anything about it at the office or the police station when I called. I wonder . . ." Then she started to shuffle papers on her desk as if looking for something, but her mind was still on the call.

Finally she turned her attention to Martin again. "Is there something you wanted?" she said, realizing he was still standing at her desk.

"Well, I was wondering," Martin said, looking as calm as he could—he was trying not to think of her as his enemy now that he had rescued Jennie—"I was wondering whether or not you think I should take Spanish next semester?"

"Well," said Miss Battaglia, "whether or not you take Spanish is up to you." Then she said, "However, I'm always interested in having students who genuinely want to learn the language. Do you have a special interest in Spanish?"

"Well, sometimes I think it might come in handy to know Spanish. I mean if you want to communicate with people in other countries," he added.

"Well, there are many Spanish-speaking people in this country. It's no longer necessary to travel to another country to use another language," the teacher replied.

"Thanks," said Martin, nodding. He tried to keep eye contact with her as he picked up his books. At the bottom of his gaze he could see the folder he was leaving on her desk. He wondered if she would notice. "Yes, thanks," he added. "I appreciate your talking to me about it. Maybe I will take it." He started toward the door quickly.

She didn't call after him. Surely if she had noticed his leaving the folder . . . As he was about to go out the door, he turned and saw that she was busy gathering up the things on her desk. He saw her reach for the folder he had left and shove it absentmindedly in with the rest. Outside the door, Martin breathed a huge sigh of relief. Then he did happy, quick, hop steps down the hall.

In Martin's mind he saw Jennie looking at her report card in amazement. "I didn't flunk," she was saying to her friend. "I actually got a C! I can still be a cheerleader!"

Martin stood watching her at a respectful distance. She will never know, he thought. "But that's all right. I'll be near whenever she needs me."

Then there entered into his mind a new dangerous situation for Jennie to face and he immediately set out to rescue her.

A young person who is constantly preoccupied with his or her daydreams or fantasies may be withdrawing from reality and using them as an escape from problems in living. Continued use of fantasies in this manner will mean the young person cannot successfully move on to adulthood. This indicates professional help may be needed. At a minimum, an evaluation of the young person's overdependence on fantasies is warranted. Also one should be alert as to whether or not the fantasies lead to constructive behavior. If they lead to destructive behavior, mental-health services should be sought.

The following Monday, Martin waited outside the Spanish class when tests were handed back. Luiz came out of the room first. "Hey, Luiz," Martin called to him. "How'd you do on your test?"

" 'A', man. Like always," Luiz shot back.

Martin smiled. Little did Luiz know it, but that meant Jennie got an A too. Martin waited for her to come out but she didn't. He peeked in the door to make sure he didn't miss her. She was up front talking to Miss Battaglia. "She's probably being congratulated on getting such a good grade," Martin thought. The bell for the next period class rang. He headed off. As long as Luiz got an A, it meant Jennie's world would be okay.

Martin tried to catch Jennie after her last class just to see the excitement and the enthusiasm on her face, but she wasn't in her last class. He thought that was strange. Even if she was feeling excited, it would be strange for her to cut class.

When Jennie didn't come to school the next morning, Martin got his courage up to ask one of the other cheerleaders where she was.

"Didn't you hear? Jennie's been suspended. Miss Battaglia thinks she cheated on her Spanish test."

"Cheat?" Martin said quickly. "Jennie would never cheat." Then, as the true meaning of it all began to sink in, Martin turned away stunned.

Suspended! God, it was unfair. The teacher had no proof. How could she know Jennie didn't pass the test all by herself? Martin was very angry all of a sudden. How dare the teacher do that to Jennie! No, it had to be the principal. He was the one who handled cases like that and decided what to do about them. He had no right to suspend her. Jennie didn't cheat.

Martin's jaw tightened. He had to find a way to get even with the principal.

LYDIA

It was nearly a week before Lydia felt that she could really go very far from her aunt's villa. It had been three days before her sunburn had healed enough for her to go to the grocery store for more canned milk and soup. Even then, during the trip her skin felt like it was on fire whenever she had to walk out from under the shadow of the buildings into the sunlight.

Now, however, she was beginning to feel both physically and emotionally that she would like to get out. Her pain and sadness had been terrible the days she stayed inside lonely and hurting. But she brightened a bit as she thought of going someplace.

An emotionally unhealthy person who becomes unhappy is more likely to feel something is wrong with the whole world rather than just the particular event or circumstance that caused him or her to feel sad. The emotionally stable person, even if he or she suffers the loss of a relative or close friend, may still be able to smile, to appreciate a beautiful sunny day or the antics of a kitten, whereas the emotionally unhealthy person is not able to do this.

On the way in from the distant airport, she noticed that not too far from her aunt's villa, in the opposite direction she had gone to the beach, was a small modern-looking resort. Other than the one guesthouse in town, it seemed to be the only tourist accommodation. Briefly, Lydia wondered how much everything would change when the giant new hotel she had seen on the way to the beach was completed. At any rate, for the first time in a long while Lydia felt she just wanted to be among people. Even in the off-season, there would have to be some tourists there. And if there were any Americans among them that would be even better.

Lydia put on an aqua-striped dress and tied her hair back neatly with a ribbon. She took out her makeup. It seemed so strange to put it on. She had not used any since she got here. She picked up a nice pair of low-heeled sandals but did not put them on. Since she could see the resort on a spit of land sticking out in the water, she decided she would walk there by way of the dirt path along the water. She tucked some foreign bills in her tiny purse and started off.

It was interesting. The land on the way to the resort was not made up of cliffs as it was on the way to the beach. The land was much flatter, and slightly rolling as it neared the water. There were gravelly sand and coral in the water with only an occasional boulder. But there was the same curved coastline. Hence she could see the resort from her aunt's home but not from the town. While she walked along the path, the resort sometimes disappeared from view as she walked inward and then reappeared as she walked outward.

As she came around a wide curve, she saw a number of men working on the hillside near the path. As she drew closer, she saw they were shoveling small rocks into burlap bags. Several donkeys stood patiently nearby. One man's donkey already had two full bags tied on its back. She stood by calmly while the man put a final shovelful in a bag that already seemed as if it could hold no more.

Lydia marveled that this seemingly small animal could carry bags filled with so many rocks. What were the rocks for? Perhaps for walls at the new hotel. Lydia wanted to feel sorry for the donkeys. But life here was so different. There were no modern machines, no refrigeration. Life was harder, more basic.

That was just the way it was—everyone seemed to accept it, even the animals. The donkeys did not look bony. Nor did they stagger or pull on their ropes and bray in resistance. Even though the men controlled the animals, Lydia felt their lives and the lives of the pack animals were not so very different.

Lydia looked at the men a little anxiously as she passed. They smiled and nodded without stopping their work. She smiled back and passed on. She felt a little more human, a bit more of a person today.

She walked in and out of two more curves. It was a truly beautiful day. Then something black on the ground caught her eye on the next stretch of flat stony land. She didn't understand what it was. The fact that she could see it from such a distance meant it had to be rather big. She strained her eyes as she walked. It didn't look like anything she could imagine. It was not the shape of driftwood and it was bigger than a log would be. It was definitely not like the boulders that occasionally erupted into sight at the water's edge.

The closer she got, the more she thought that it looked like birds standing on land not too far from the water's edge. Finally she realized that's what it was. "Yes, I'm right. They're large black birds. Lots and lots of big black birds." She had never seen birds like that; they were as tall as her knees. And they appeared to be just standing, not moving. Lots of big birds, just standing there.

The closer Lydia got, the more she had a feeling of uneasiness. Big black birds would not be standing near the water in such a large number for no reason. There must be something going on. She strained her eyes again, a little fearful of what she would see.

Soon she saw something gray among the feet of the birds. As she drew closer, she began to make out the shape of an animal. It was a donkey, lying on its side. Its eyes were open. Lydia hoped it was dead. Its coat was still wet with water. The sun had not dried it, so it had not been washed up for long. Yet it had obviously been there long enough for the huge birds to congregate.

Lydia was frightened by the stillness. The birds were still not moving. Some seemed to stare at the water. Others the hills. Others stared at nowhere in particular. They just stood there in great numbers, all motionless.

Then Lydia saw a bird dart and pull something red and stringy from the donkey's anus. It gobbled it down quickly. Then there was no movement again. Finally another bird moved in, pecked at the donkey's eye and moved back quickly. Again no movement. Another rushed to the donkey's side and pulled a bit of red flesh from an almost unobservable hole.

Lydia turned her eyes away and began to run up the beach in the direction of the resort hotel. They were picking at the most vulnerable parts of the donkey as it lay there helpless. It was dead, she was sure now, but it was helpless nevertheless. It was being violated by those awful flesh-eating black birds. Lydia hated the birds.

The beach curved back inland again. Lydia slowed as she rounded the curve. She could no longer see the resort but it must be only three or four more curves away. Suddenly, out of the corner of her eyes she caught a flash of green. A young, slightly built boy probably not much older than she was, wearing a green shirt and brown loose pants, was coming down the hillside towards her. Instantly she stiffened. Without thinking she knew what he was coming down for.

Lydia looked ahead. The resort was no longer visible. She looked behind, hoping that the men shoveling rocks into the donkeys' packs were in sight. They weren't. The land curved in such a way they were out of sight.

"I must just keep going forward as fast as I can," she thought. "I must not panic." She felt her heels digging into the dirt on the path. Maybe walking in the water is faster, she thought, splashing in up to her ankles on the pebbles.

Now the boy was at her side. He murmured something and made a gesture in front of his pants with his hands. She shook her head no. He grabbed her arm and said something again. His eyes were gleaming and he was smiling.

"No." she said, pushing him away, "no."

He grabbed at her and she began to run. Her purse fell from her hands. He caught her. She shoved at him and broke his hold. But he grabbed her again. He was trying to force her down. She spun around and partially freed herself. But he grabbed her again and reached to feel her dress. She was amazed how weak she was. Her diet of crackers and canned milk and soup had left her thin.

She went down on her knees but struggled up to her feet again. She was off balance, however, and fell sideways against him. She could feel his hands on her. If only I could stop thinking. She wanted to turn her mind off so that she didn't have to know what was going on. Stop thinking, she thought to herself, stop thinking. She struggled even harder.

Where is help? Where is anyone? She thought of Wayne. Oh where was he? He had once rescued her when she felt she was nowhere and had no one. Where was Wayne? He was nowhere. There was no one. There was no help. There was only the whole empty busy world. In her were the last little vestiges of self, thinking, being aware, and not being able to shut off.

The struggle continued. The boy pinned Lydia's arms; she tried to kick him. When he moved away and she freed her arms, he grabbed her elsewhere. He attempted to kiss her face as his hands felt her body. She bit his lip and nose. He became angry and she struggled in greater fear.

How long can this go on? she thought. They struggled back and forth. Twice she fell down, but before he could pin her she got back up. She was wet and dirty—much more so than he was. Finally, with a grin and a final feeling up of her body he turned and started off. Fearfully, she grabbed her sandals and started to run back the way she had come, sobbing as she went. She wished she had something to wipe the dirt off her face. It was gritty and it hurt. Her arms and hands were just as dirty. Her clothes clung to her and were covered with the same brown, clingy, pebbly mud.

She stopped to pick up her purse and tried to brush the dirt off her watch. There was water in the case. "Oh my watch," she thought. "Mom gave that to me for graduation from junior high school." She glanced back at the hillside. There was no sign of the boy now.

She must get back to the villa, must get out of her clothes. She had to get back to safety. She moved quickly around a curve.

Then she saw it again. The dead donkey and the birds who were busier now. "No, no," she gasped. "All alone, so weak . . . when you are helpless, that's when they come, when you are alone." Her feeling of being alone in the world took on a new meaning. Before she had felt alone with the outside world shut out. Now she understood the outside world was not passive but waiting for its chance at her.

The trip back seemed long. She got to the place where the

men had been loading the donkeys with stones. She was glad they weren't there to see her humiliation. Several more turns and she saw the roof of her aunt's villa.

Lydia pulled out the door key from her wet purse and unlocked the door. She stepped into the house and stood there whimpering like an injured animal. Then she became aware again of how muddy and wet she was.

She went into the bath area. She caught sight of her dress in the mirror. She couldn't stand the sight or feel of it because he had touched it. She quickly pulled it off, the small pebbles scraping and hurting her skin as she did. She threw it on the floor of the shower. She turned on the water, stepped in, and let the water run over her, over her dress, for a long time. There would never be enough water to do what she needed to have done. The water turned cold. She stood in the cold stream until her body could no longer stand it. Then she wrapped herself in a blanket and got into bed.

It almost didn't matter that she had not been raped. The humiliation of his assault overwhelmed her. You can't stop thinking. You can't stop thinking when it happens, she thought. She was living the incident over. You are so aware of everything that's going on. You can't stop thinking.

All night she lay thinking, unable to sleep, shivering. The world became black around her and the black lay inside her in endless empty corridors.

Lydia stayed in bed the next morning. At noon she forced herself to get up and drink a warm soda. She picked her dress up off the floor of the shower and forced herself to wash it out in the sink and hang it up to dry. Then she got back into bed.

The whole world now seemed so much smaller, so closed off. What would she do now? She could no longer go for her exploration hikes. Yet she could not just be locked in the villa. Damn everything. Damn life, damn death, damn the hell in between.

Lydia felt she couldn't go back home to her family. She had come too far. There was nothing back there for her. She lay in bed and looked out the window at the roof of the small villa next door. Time passed. There were clay pots sitting on the other villa's roof. Their color seemed to change, but ever so slightly as the sun moved downward in the sky. Finally a cat came up the roof through the trees and vines in the center courtyard of the villa. The cat stretched, and walked around the pots. The sun went down further. The pots turned purple in the light. The tree leaves hung without moving. The cat disappeared. Lydia's room began to darken also.

What had it all meant? What did anything mean? There was nowhere to go, nothing to do. The light dimmed further. Lydia was alone in the dark and she began to cry. Anyone who has ever cried as hard as Lydia would remember crying like that forever.

GEORGE

George couldn't believe he'd done it. He had gotten into a fist fight with Brodie. And Brodie was his best friend!

A bunch of the kids from school had gone to the softball field for a Saturday morning game. It was strictly for fun so George didn't mind that they had more girls on his team. Actually some of the girls played pretty well, but for George it basically meant there were more girls to horse around with.

George was trying to put his old baseball cap on some of the girls. One girl wouldn't let him and kept dodging away screaming. She said she was going someplace that night and was trying to keep her hair looking nice. Finally George was able to grab her. Then Brodie started defending the girl. He told George to leave her alone and tried to lead George away. George started to struggle with Brodie, and before he knew it he had hit Brodie hard in the eye. George hadn't intended to do that, but he didn't like Brodie telling him what to do.

But to hit his best friend hard in the eye? No way. Anyway, that broke up the game. It really soured the morning for everyone.

Then the girl with the hairdo decided to leave and take Brodie with her in her car because he'd stuck up for her. That meant George had no one in his car. Since he felt badly about what he'd done, he didn't want to ask anyone to ride with him.

There are many people who do not have major mental or emotional disturbances and cannot be called neurotic or psychotic. However, minor mental-health problems may lead them to be quick to pick fights, be excessively negative and dissatisfied with everything, or be jittery or grumpy. This behavior can hinder them in their personal relationships or keep them from being successful in school or in their jobs.

Instead, George got in his car alone and screeched out of the parking lot heading south. He didn't know where he would go. "God, why did I do that?" he thought. "I mean, what was the big deal about getting the girls to wear my baseball cap? It was fun but I really didn't have to do it."

And why did he fight with Brodie? They were best friends. Normally Brodie picked up George and drove him everywhere, because even though George's father had let him get his driver's license, he rarely let him have the car. If it weren't for Brodie, George wouldn't have gotten to go half the places he had.

That day Brodie's car was on the fritz, so George had talked his mom into borrowing the car for the day and promised to have it back by the time his dad got home from his golfing date. George knew when his dad played in the afternoons he always had some drinks with his buddies before coming home, which made him later than when he just played in the morning.

Actually George's mother did not have the power to let him take the car, for his dad thought that was a decision he alone should make. However, if George got the car back before his dad knew, his dad would never know he had taken it.

———————

Young people are sometimes aware that they need limits and are grateful to their parents for setting them. Parental limits on where young people can go or what they can do, for example, are often used by young people to refrain from doing things they might otherwise do, against their better judgment. Due to the experimentation and sorting out process that are normal in adolescence, young people often cannot set their own limits. Some become upset or scared if they feel the limits are not clear or if they have greater freedom than they feel comfortable in handling. As a consequence they may engage in behavior that will in the end force adults to set limits.

———————

George barreled down the highway. He was all set to have a good time with Brodie that day but he'd messed up in the first half hour and now had the rest of the day with nothing to do. Plus he had packed his bathing suit on the chance they decided to go to the beach after the game.

George wanted company. Part of the fun of having the car was to breeze around with a friend. He thought of who he could get to go along with him this afternoon. Suddenly he thought of Marilyn. He had heard she was back from her vacation in Florida. She wasn't working this summer either because she was taking French in summer school.

George's mouth grew tight at the thought of the yelling

he and his dad had done over his getting a job over the summer. A lot of kids had been out looking for jobs during the time George was grounded. Then with other things being what they were, George had just not picked up on it the minute his grounding ended. By the time he started job-hunting, most of the good ones had been filled. The one he most wanted—being a lifeguard at the lake—had been grabbed by Phillip Smythe. That kid got everything. He got his own brand new car on his seventeenth birthday—not just permission to get a driver's license like George but his own brand new car! Of course his folks were richer than George's; but it wasn't the wealth, it was the idea that Phillip's parents wanted him to have a brand new car at seventeen. His own dad probably wouldn't even want him to have one at twenty-five. And now Phillip had the job at the beach too. Shit!

Anyway as the summer approached and George hadn't gotten a job, his father rode him harder. He kept telling him about the ways he used to hustle to get jobs when he was young. Finally when one of the places George had applied to did offer him a job, George was so hopping mad he just told the man he didn't want it. Of course George didn't tell his father this, because that would have capped everything. Instead, he secretly enjoyed the fact that his father didn't know he could have had a job but didn't take it. Anyway, that job was not something George would have enjoyed doing. But here he was with nothing to do all summer. So he had to think up his own existence each day.

George turned off the highway, took a shortcut through some back streets and arrived at Marilyn's house. He was surprised when she answered the door herself. There was an awkward silence. Then George said, "I heard you were back. It's such a neat day I thought you might enjoy a drive to the lake."

"Gee, George," Marilyn said, first looking at George closely to make sure he wasn't stoned and then peering around him at the car. "I don't know. My mom's gone to the beauty parlor and I didn't tell her I was going to go anyplace."

"C'mon," said George in his most persuading tone. "Look, it's an absolutely incredible day. I told my mom I'd have the car home by 5:30 at the latest so we won't be gone all that long. Besides, I'd like to see Phillip on his lifeguard perch."

George looked at Marilyn innocently. He knew after he and Marilyn had stopped going steady she had started dating Phillip Smythe. Phillip was so good-looking and had so much charm that all the girls wanted to date him. But George also knew to Phillip the grass was always greener on the other side and he could never stick with just one girl. So George wasn't surprised when a month or so after Phillip started to date Marilyn, he started dating someone else too. To George's knowledge Marilyn had always stopped dating boys before they stopped dating her. George guessed Marilyn might just like to appear at the beach with a date and then drive off leaving Phillip on his perch.

George wanted to see Phillip in his lifeguard chair over-looking the beach too—but for a different reason. The thought of Phillip having to stay in his chair while all those girls in bikinis lay on the beach out his reach must be some sort of exquisite torture to Phillip.

Sure George knew that girls went for lifeguards (which, to tell the truth, was one of the reasons that George had wanted the job). However, lifeguards had to stay serious and not fool around. It must be rough, in a way, having to sit in the chair and watch other guys make out with their girls on the beach.

"Well, okay," Marilyn was saying. "If you are sure we'll be back no later than 5:30. I'd really rather be back before my mom gets home."

"Well, I gotta be back before my dad gets home, so no problem," George said.

"Give me just a sec," Marilyn said, and disappeared into the house.

George smiled on the way down to the car. This was the first time he had asked Marilyn to go anywhere since their big breakup. Maybe this would lead to their getting back together. She sure was pretty. And he did like her a lot. Dating was important. If only Marilyn weren't so bossy.

As Marilyn got into the car she said to George, "How's your sister doing?"

George frowned. Why did she have to bring that up? He supposed she was just being polite but it made him kinda mad. Ruining a good afternoon talking about Geraldine.

"She's out of the hospital and home, if that's what you mean," George said sharply. Of course there was no way to keep folks from knowing she had been in the hospital. But it was awfully embarrassing to know other people knew he had this weirdo for a sister.

"Well, is she all right now?" Marilyn persisted.

George knew Marilyn was asking out of real concern but it rubbed him the wrong way anyway. "Who the hell knows," George said abruptly, turning on the engine, "and who the hell cares." He spun the car's tires as he sped away from the curb. Marilyn settled back in her seat with a frown on her face.

Sometimes therapy does not go as well as the adolescent, the parent, or the mental-health practitioner hopes. The parent or adolescent can discuss this with the therapist. They can also get an opinion from another therapist. No therapy is better than bad therapy. Therefore, if need be, the adolescent can discontinue with the mental-health practitioner and seek help elsewhere. However, a thorough evaluation should be done before discontinuing, to assure that the person needing mental-health assistance is leaving for the right reasons.

Therapists are people, too, and sometimes the personalities just do not fit. Or sometimes the patient's problem doesn't fit the type of therapy the mental-health professional is prepared to offer.

———————

By the time they got to the beach both George and Marilyn were in a better mood. It really was a nice day and the thought of seeing some of their friends appealed to both of them.

Sure enough, Phillip was on his lifeguard perch. George noticed that the minute Marilyn assured herself that Phillip was up there, she made an obvious point of walking over to her friends without even glancing at him. George said "Hi" to Marilyn's friends and put his towel down next to hers. Then he walked over to the lifeguard stand.

"Well, Phillip, how is it living in a bird's nest all summer?"

"Hot," said Phillip, smiling and glancing down at George.

"Rescued any beautiful girls?" George asked.

"No, but I did get a beach ball for a five-year old."

"Great stuff," George replied.

"Yes," said Phillip. "Now I'm the idol of millions of kindergarteners."

George talked on with Phillip. That was the trouble with the guy. He was conceited but he had every right to be. He had a neat personality, which meant you couldn't help but like him. Besides, he really was handsome and rich and talented.

"George!" He heard Marilyn calling as she went toward the water with a couple of girls. She didn't look at Phillip.

"Well, listen man, I've got to get back to Marilyn," George said. "I'll probably see you again. I expect Marilyn will want to parade back and forth a couple of times in front of you before we leave." George looked up at Phillip and cocked his head. Phillip grinned back. They exchanged looks that said guys know a lot about girls and we both know Marilyn.

George started off after Marilyn. She had already waded in up to her waist. In another minute she'd be swimming.

Just then another voice called to George. "Hey, George, over here!" George was surprised to see Donnie and another boy he didn't recognize. They turned and motioned George to follow them around the bathhouse.

"George, my man," Donnie said, "we were just about to roll some joints." They offered George the makings.

George hesitated. He hadn't had any for awhile and some part of him said, "Don't do it." On the other hand, another part of him said, "Go ahead, you don't get many chances these days. Besides, you don't want these guys to think you've turned chicken after the drug bust."

The adolescent who is using drugs may need help in giving up the drugs. One way to do this is to help him or her find in reality an answer which heretofore he or she may only have found in using drugs. The adolescent may have to be helped to experience the "natural highs" available in life and to determine which ones he or she wants to make more central to their existence. Natural highs for some people include listening to music, doing sports such as running, meaningful conversation, and mastering skills such as woodworking. Or the adolescent may need help in developing new ways of confronting those life problems that are making his or her existence so uncomfortable that they seek escape. Or the adolescent may simply need help and support in dealing with the peer-group pressure that leads young people to do things they might not otherwise do.

George rolled a reefer and began to smoke. After the first few puffs he felt more relaxed and less anxious about having some pot. However, he wanted to get back to Marilyn, so when someone else joined the group he turned his joint over to him and went to look for Marilyn. She was just coming out of the water.

"Where have you been?" she demanded. "I thought you were coming in."

"I had to go back by the johns," George replied. He wasn't lying. He was back by the johns. "C'mon in again," he said, picking Marilyn up and carrying her kicking back into the water. They swam together and played around awhile and then she said she wanted to sunbathe. George watched her get out and go up the beach. She had a really neat figure. If only she weren't so bossy.

George lay back on the water and just floated. The grass made him conscious of the gentle wave-motion of the water in a totally new way. He looked at the clouds and saw them as he had never seen them before. His mind wandered in strange convoluted ways through the sky.

All of a sudden he found himself coughing and sputtering out water. He must have relaxed so much he let himself slip under the water. He was still coughing as he came out. He must have swallowed a lot of water. Yuk. He knew the little kids always peed in the water. He had done that too as a kid.

As he passed near the lifeguard stand, Phillip called to him. "Hey, what were you doing out there? I thought you were going to be the first person for me to rescue this summer."

George was still coughing, so he just motioned to Phillip with his hand as he went past. Finally catching his breath, he sat down beside Marilyn.

"George, you look awful," Marilyn said when she looked up.

"Oh, I just swallowed some lake water and it went down the wrong way," George said. He turned on his stomach and lay next to Marilyn, but turned his face away from her. Grass certainly did not make him feel oversexed.

George must have dozed off because he came to with Marilyn shaking him.

"Look, if we're going to get home by 5:30," she said, "we better start back now."

"Oh," said George groggily. "Let's not go home yet. This is too wonderful . . ." He stretched and rolled over.

"George, you promised," Marilyn said.

George got up slowly and, folding his towel, started back toward the car. He remembered to turn and wave goodbye to Phillip as he left but found that Phillip's attention was directed elsewhere.

He felt moody. He really would much rather stay at the lake. It was not so hot now. As a matter of fact, this was the perfect time of day to be at the beach as far as he was concerned. Damn his father and his restrictions on the car. Why couldn't George just use it when he wanted and as long as he wanted? At least on days like today when his father was not going to use it at all.

Oh well, he would be home when he said he would. At any rate his mother would appreciate that. He backed the car carefully out of the parking space and drove slowly out of the parking lot. Because he had smoked he wanted to make sure he was cautious driving home. "I can drive perfectly normally," he said to himself. "I just want to be careful, that's all. No point in having anything happen."

But then something did happen. A dog ran out in the road and the car coming the other way swerved toward George to avoid it. George tried to avoid the other car. It was doubtful even under normal circumstances whether he could have swerved away from the other car, but his reflexes under the drug were a little slower than normal. He sideswiped the other car, ran off the road, and came to a dead stop against a telephone pole which promptly cracked and fell over backwards with the impact.

George realized Marilyn was crying and holding her arm. The front end of the car was crumpled. In the rear-view mirror, George saw the unhurt dog running off into a field. "Damn bastard," he swore.

Several hours later George sat in the emergency waiting room of the hospital waiting for his parents to come pick him up. He hadn't been hurt but Marilyn had a broken arm.

Although Marilyn didn't seem to be mad at him, her parents were. He would never forget the look they gave him when they came to take her home. It had made him feel really terrible—like he was some kind of untrustworthy kid. It hadn't been his fault. The other car had swerved into his path. After they left he felt like he was at the bottom of the barrel.

While waiting for his own parents to come, George had a lot of time to think. He saw a drunk brought in with a head wound. The guy had fallen over and hit his head. He was a bum but they fussed over him just the same. George saw a child brought in who had eaten prescription medicine out of her mother's purse because it looked like colored candy. The mother didn't know how many the three-year-old had taken. George could hear the child screaming as they unsuccessfully tried to get her to swallow the medicine that would make her vomit. George saw an old woman with a heart condition brought in. All these people seemed so disconnected with his life. He wanted to feel superior to them but couldn't.

What am I doing here? he wondered. How did I get here? Things just aren't going right for me anymore. He sat morosely on one of the uncomfortable orange chairs. A resident wandered in to take a break. He sat down next to George and made small talk about the emergency room and the kinds of cases they treated.

For no reason at all George suddenly asked, "Do psychiatrists really help people?"

The resident studied him a minute and said, "I think they do."

"I think I want to see one," George said.

"Well, we don't have a psychiatrist in the emergency room."

"I know," George mumbled. "It's just something I want to do."

"Wait here," the resident said. George watched as the doctor walked over to a phone. He seemed to have made three calls. Finally he returned with a hospital card.

"I've made an appointment for you with one of the psychologists who works here part-time. That's not exactly the same thing as a psychiatrist but he'll know if you need to see a psychiatrist. His hospital time was booked up far in advance, so he gave you an appointment at his private office. He'll discuss fees before he talks with you. At any rate I know him personally and can recommend him. He's a pretty good guy. As a matter of fact, I wish I'd had someone like him to talk to a couple of times in my life."

George looked at the resident in surprise. He thought doctors had it all together. For some reason it never occurred to him that doctors were people who might have life problems too.

George took the hospital card. The psychologist's office address and phone number were handwritten on the back with the appointment time. "Thanks," he said.

"Don't mention it. Well, I better get back inside and check on patients. Take care." The resident strode slowly through the doors marked "No Admittance. Emergency Room."

Adolescents may decide they need help because they feel things are not going right and don't know what to do to make things better. Adolescents may feel everything is going downhill, or they feel lost or confused. In general people seek help for a variety of reasons. They may be concerned because they are feeling depressed, inadequate, hopeless, guilty, frightened, distrustful of people, incapable of making even small decisions, forgetful, preoccupied with certain ideas, or they are having frightening thoughts, considering suicide. They may be concerned that they cannot get along with others, that they get into fights too often, get in trouble with the law too much, cannot keep good relationships, are dependent on drugs or alcohol, cry a lot, cannot sleep well, sleep too much, or have terrible nightmares. Other people may experience the same things as minor troubles, and may be able to cope with them on their own. Others, however, experience them as major ones for which immediate help is needed. Most people are surprised that after only a short time with a mental-health professional, their feelings and attitudes about life improve in significant ways.

George looked at the card in his hand. It seemed strange to him. It made him feel even more disconnected with his own life, more out of sync with things. The doctor had said this man was a pretty good guy, but what would George say to him? Could anybody do anything about anything?

A commotion in the entry way caused him to look up. Before he even saw who it was, he guessed. It was his father striding toward him, eyes flashing. George shoved the hospital card hastily into his pants pocket but kept his hand there tightly curled around the card. It was as if he needed to hang on to it while he endured the explosion that was about to occur.

6

Will You Listen?
Will I Listen?

MARTIN

Everything to Martin seemed so messed up. The principal's secretary had caught him attaching wires to the principal's desk chair. Since Martin wouldn't talk to anyone about what he was doing or why, he had been sent to the school social worker who referred him to a county mental-health clinic. Martin would not have gone, but by that time his parents were involved and they insisted. It took forever to get all the paperwork done and Martin had to wait in crowded waiting rooms with smelly people, some of whom acted very strangely.

"We've got a very fine youth program," one of the people there told his mother apologetically. "I'm sorry, it just takes a bit of doing to get the paperwork done and the arrangements made. Unless it's a real crisis, it really is hard to expedite this stuff. Even then, we don't always do as well as we should."

Anyone seeking mental-health treatment will want certain information. For example, they will want the person providing the mental-health service to define why he or she believes treatment is appropriate, what it will involve, if

137

there are any alternative ways to treat the problem, how much treatment will cost, and how long it will take. The person seeking mental-health treatment will also want to know if there are any risks involved (particularly with the use of drugs), how treatment can be stopped, or what will determine if treatment is no longer needed. Both adolescents and their parents have a right to know these things.

Martin's mother seemed to have more patience than he did. But then Martin understood more about what was going on than his mother. He wasn't crazy. And no one would understand about Jennie, particularly some dumb shrink. There would be nothing to talk about, even when he got to whoever he was supposed to see. His mother assured everyone they came in contact with that she and his father would be glad to come and to talk to anyone at anytime about anything.

Martin sighed. That was his mother. She was always overly helpful . . . She was hard working and he loved her. He felt badly she was involved in all this.

Family therapy is often used if several members of a family need help with mutual problems. Sometimes it is easier to solve conflicts if everyone involved can work on it together. The therapist's role may be to help family members understand each other's feelings better or to note how they interact and then help them become more aware of the things they do that lead to conflict. Family members who are given this new awareness can then try to change their behavior.

It was funny. Things that were so in order and so real to Martin inside his head always came out sounding different—

a bit funny when he tried to tell them to others, even his parents. And there were just some things he couldn't talk about with his parents. They were comfortable sorts of people and he liked them. But they were his parents. They just wouldn't understand. He wasn't even sure that they could. He was sorry to confuse and disappoint them. They were really nice people.

Martin's first visit with the student mental-health worker was a disaster. Martin wouldn't talk and nothing the student did seemed to open him up. Martin felt he was a very private person and his relationship with Jennie a very personal and private one. He had no intention of talking about either himself or Jennie with this person, or any other person for that matter. I'm not crazy, Martin thought. I've always felt different. But I'm not crazy. Or maybe I am crazy and I just don't know it. Anyway, I have no desire to talk to any of the people here.

It surprised Martin when, at the end of their time, the student smiled and said good-naturedly, "Well, I guess I'll have to go talk to my supervisor about you. I sure haven't been of any help to you today at all. Maybe he can give me some ideas about how to be a better helper next time."

Martin felt rather sorry for the student. He hadn't meant to make it difficult for him.

Whether or not the supervisor gave the student some tips, Martin didn't know, but the next time he found it easier to talk to him. Eventually he even got up enough courage to mention Jennie. But when he tried to explain about some of the things that had gone on, it didn't sound quite real, even to Martin. Martin tried to figure out if things had really been the way he first remembered them, if that was reality and this was just a skewed perspective, or if things hadn't been quite real back then and the way he saw them now was the reality.

---

*There are various methods of treatment that therapists
use in helping those who come to them with problems. No
one method is generally accepted as the best for all problems.
Therefore many therapists use several methods depending on
the situation. A very brief description of just some of the
therapies follows:*

Psychoanalysis: *Most psychotherapy methods grew out of
psychoanalysis, which was developed by Sigmund Freud. In
psychoanalysis, the person seeking help is enabled to understand the reasons for his or her behavior—and their childhood antecedents—and to emotionally accept the understanding.
The person giving this treatment does not interact with his
or her patient in ways that reveal anything about himself
or herself. Psychoanalysis is a lengthy process, often taking
years.*

Insight-oriented psychotherapy *is also based on the no-
tion that understanding ideas and feelings the patient is not
currently aware of will allow the patient to change his or
her behavior. Less emphasis is placed on childhood difficulties. The person giving this treatment may interact more
directly with the client. This therapy may be used for short-
term treatment, such as a few sessions to help someone with
a crisis, or long-term treatment involving many sessions over
time for major changes in behavior.*

Nondirective client-centered *approaches focus more on
current thoughts and feelings rather than on past events to
explain a client's problems. The therapist may share events
from his or her own life in order to help the client understand
or speak more freely about his or her life.*

Behavioral therapy *approaches mental-health difficulties
from the point of view of the person's behavior. The therapist
can help the client change his or her behavior by helping
him or her become less affected by things that bother him or*

her (desensitization), helping him or her feel rewarded by certain actions (reward), or by helping him or her feel great dislike for certain behaviors (aversive conditioning).

Transactional analysis *is based on the idea that people have child, parent, and adult aspects to their personalities. The therapist helps the person seeking treatment understand other people's behavior and his or her own behavior.*

Gestalt therapies *focus on the present as opposed to the past. The therapist tries to help the client deal with conflicts as they occur rather than leave them unresolved.*

The student worker urged Martin to become part of a young people's therapy group that the mental-health center was running. Martin felt reluctant to do so. He had always felt somewhat isolated from the kids at school and the idea of joining a group was uncomfortable for him. Finally, however, the worker was so insistent that Martin acquiesced. The worker promised he would continue to talk with Martin privately as long as they both felt that was beneficial.

The first time Martin saw his therapy group he was surprised. Somehow he had expected to find unattractive kids and real crazies. But many of the kids looked and acted pretty much like the popular kids in his school. As he learned more about them, he found out each one was having some real problems in living that kept them from enjoying life as they thought they should, or kept getting them into trouble with others. Martin identified more with the shy insecure kids in the group than he did with those who were aggressive and manipulative. He was surprised how quickly he was able to figure out how each one's style of acting and relating was working against rather than for him or her. This caused Martin to think a lot about himself and his style of living and acting.

Group therapies often use techniques that are drawn from a variety of psychotherapy methods. Group leaders may be trained professionals or lay leaders. Groups led by lay leaders (people without formal training in the helping professions) can be very effective, such as Recovery, Inc., an organization for former mental patients, and AA (Alcoholics Anonymous). Adolescent mental-health groups can be useful in giving adolescents the sense that they are not alone in dealing with problems. Adolescents can relate to and help each other in such groups.

The group spent a lot of time talking about relationships and what relating to someone meant. It was hard for Martin to give up the idea he had a relationship with Jennie. But, Martin came to see he really didn't have a relationship with her, in the way the group defined relationships. Their relationship was a one-way street and she wasn't on the street half the time.

Privately, he began to talk with the student counselor about his fantasies. The counselor reassured him that everyone had fantasies and that many young people had more violent, bizarre fantasies than he. Usually fantasies weren't harmful to people and, in fact, could be very helpful.

But, the counselor went on to explain, what was harmful was if the person spent so much time with his or her fantasies he or she began to confuse them with reality.

Martin began to become painfully aware that he had indeed confused his dreams with reality. Hardest of all was for him to give up the idea that Jennie needed him. The counselor talked to Martin about what a putdown it was to Jennie for him to assume that she couldn't deal with her own problems, that she needed someone to constantly make life right for her. For example, he pointed out that Jennie had made a mistake with the shoes, but if she never learned to live with her mistakes, she would be dependent all her life on someone to rescue her and would never be able to cope on her own. Further, he said, bailing Jennie out with the test was not really good for her. She needed to study Spanish harder, and not to have Martin cheat for her. Martin wondered if he had really interfered with Jennie's life in a bad way.

Most mental-health difficulties are caused by an interrelationship of variables and not by one single identifiable factor. In the mental-health field it is possible to treat some problems without knowing the cause of them. However, the more causes can be understood, the more likely better methods of prevention of mental-health problems can be developed. Because of this, investigators are looking closely at biological causes, genetic causes, and psychological and social causes. They are looking at how factors in each of these areas might interact with one another to bring about certain types of problems for individuals. Until more is known, blaming one thing or another for one's mental-health difficulties is probably not useful. Instead, families probably should concentrate on finding quality treatment.

As Martin tried to sort through what had happened that led him into doing some of the things he did and, in particular, how to think and feel about Jennie now, his pattern changed at school. He used to try to hang out wherever he thought he might see Jennie. Now he avoided her at all cost. Jennie was back in school—reinstated partly through the action of her parents and their insistence that since the handwriting on the test was obviously not Jennie's, the school had no grounds to assume she had cheated.

Martin hoped no one would ever find out he'd done it. If they did, he'd again be the laughingstock of the school. Just like the time he had run out of gas trying to do something serious, the girls got off but he got laughed at—even though it was the girls who asked him for the ride. And even though it was Jennie not him, who was flunking Spanish, he'd be the target of jokes.

Therefore Martin was upset when he saw Jennie coming down a hall toward him a few weeks later, especially since he had carefully taken that route to avoid her. He tried to turn into another corridor before they passed. To his astonishment she caught up with him.

"Martin, meet me," she said as she thrust a note in his hand.

At one point in his life, Jennie's giving him a note and asking him to meet her would have been a wonderful fairy tale come true, or at least the trigger for endless spectacular dreams. But now it was more like a nightmare. He didn't want to talk with Jennie. What she had to say to him could only be bad. Martin felt miserable.

All day Martin debated what to do about her note. Should he forget meeting her at the place she mentioned in the note? Should he try to find her and give her another note saying he couldn't come? Should he go and meet her and get over with whatever it was? Martin was still undecided when the last bell rang.

Slowly he began walking toward the spot where she said she would meet him. However, he had cold feet before he got there and started going in the opposite direction. To his embarrassment, he ran into Jennie on her way to meet him.

"Martin," Jennie said, immediately realizing that he had not intended to meet her. "Please, I want to talk with you."

Martin stopped and nodded unhappily and then turned and followed her. She led the way to some empty seats in the music room.

"Martin, it was you who cheated on my test, wasn't it?" Jennie looked at him directly as she asked.

Martin didn't say anything.

"And it was you who gave me the shoes, wasn't it?"

Martin looked down at his hands as they lay uselessly in his lap. He didn't know what to say. He thought back and remembered all his dreams. He heard her say: "And it was you who rescued me from the tornado, and saved my home, and got me away from the Mafia, and got me off the sabotaged jet in time, and . . ."

Then reality came back to him and Martin knew clearly the test and the shoes were the things he had done, not the other things.

"Yes," Martin said quietly. "How'd you find out?"

Jennie said, "The minute Miss Battaglia showed me the test and I saw it wasn't my handwriting, I started to think about who it could be. And somehow 'cause you were always hanging around where I was and I used to see you watching me . . ."

Martin winced at the thought he had been so obvious about everything.

"I knew that it had to be you," she finished.

"I suppose you told everyone I did it," Martin said.

"Of course not," Jennie said indignantly. "Why would I do a thing like that?" Then she added, "I just want to know why you did it."

Martin sat miserably quiet. Could he tell her she was the most wonderful girl in the world, or at least had been, that he had been wildly in love with her, and about his illusion of her needing him. He struggled with his thoughts. But, somehow, now she wasn't that way to him, things weren't like that to him. Since he had been in the mental-health group, a lot of things seemed different. In some ways it was even hard to remember what it had been like when he had had just pure dreams about Jennie. Now it was all complicated by his different understanding of himself, of relationships, and what in life was hard for him.

"Well, Martin," Jennie said. "Maybe it doesn't matter why you did it. I guess you meant well. But I just wanted to tell you not to do anything anymore. Okay? I don't want someone else manipulating things for me. I just want to live my life on my own. Okay?" Jennie looked directly at Martin as she said this. But he still did not look back at her.

Martin's head was whirling. If she was asking him not to do it again, then she hadn't told the principal. If she had, the principal might have told the teachers and Miss Battaglia might have remembered the calls, the car tires, the honey, and then things would be in a worse mess than ever. But then, of course, Jennie wouldn't know about the latter and would think she was just telling about the test or the shoes.

Martin looked at her. So she had figured out it was him, but she was the only one who knew. She hadn't told the principal and hadn't told her friends. She was just telling him. She hadn't told anyone about him, even though he really had caused her a lot of trouble, getting her temporarily suspended and all that.

The full impact was dawning on him. She was keeping what had gone on a secret and was only telling him and asking him not to do it anymore. Martin tried to think of what to say. The real Jennie was turning out to be a very special person. Very few of her girlfriends would do what she was doing, he thought. They were all gossips.

Martin looked at Jennie sitting next to him waiting for an answer. This was not the fantasy Jennie—the lovely helpless one who relied on him for everything. This was a really strong person who wanted to manage her life herself.

"Thanks, Jennie," Martin said simply.

"Thanks for what?" Jennie said curiously.

"For turning out to be who you are."

"Look," Jennie said, not understanding. "All I'm asking is for you not to do those things."

"I won't," said Martin. "Not again. I promise. That part is over."

"Okay," said Jennie. "That's all I wanted." She stood up and looked at him. He could tell she was struggling for some way to end their meeting.

Finally she said, "I have to go now. Thanks for meeting with me. And, don't worry, I really won't tell anyone."

Martin watched her walk off. He sat thinking for quite awhile and then decided to head for home.

As Martin got to the front of the school, he saw Jennie walking with Peter Dunkin. He really wasn't surprised. He knew they had been dating recently. He supposed they were very close. But something about his conversation with Jennie let him know that as close as she and Peter Dunkin were or might become, she would not tell on him.

Martin smiled. How weird. He ended up sharing a secret with Jennie, a secret that was born out of his past fantasies about her which were not true. The counselor was right. It had been so easy to mix fantasy and reality before. He didn't quite know now how he could have forgotten which was reality, but was sure now what it was.

"No more, Jennie," he promised out loud. "Not for you nor for anybody." With that he continued on home, pausing only now and then to think. "She figured it out. She didn't like it but she didn't tell anyone. She's so different than I thought."

LYDIA

The morning sky was gray when Lydia awoke, one of the few times she had seen it that way. On the ground was a strong breeze. The chill of the wind annoyed Lydia. Since she felt so little warmth inside she needed the sun to heat her body each day.

Lydia decided to go into town. Today, however, there was no one relaxing on the stone wall overlooking the water. Nor was there anyone sauntering down the streets. Even the normally gay Dairy Queen had a lonely desolate look about it.

Lydia walked aimlessly down the streets. The whitewashed walls of the few buildings comprising the town were sterile and boring. Lydia quickly reached the other end of town. There was nothing to do but to go back to the villa although it held nothing for her.

However, as she turned to start back Lydia was startled to see a huge vessel anchored not far from shore. It had evidently come in during the night, and was riding very low in the water. She walked quickly toward the water. The shoreline was filled with activity. Flatbed trucks had pulled up as close as they could to the water. Men in sturdy wooden boats rowed to and from the ship like ants going back and forth to a dropped piece of food.

Lydia became aware of the isolation of the area in a new way. As yet there was no road from the capital city over the mountains to this area. The only way in was by plane as she had done. But of course, large items or loads had to come by ship. And without a deep harbor or dock, a ship could only anchor offshore and have its cargo brought in by smaller boats.

Lydia walked along the upper road until she came to a place where she could descend to the rocky shore to watch more closely. A crane on the deck of the freighter swung brown burlap bags down to the waiting boats in a sling. The sling was then unfastened, and the process was repeated till the small boat was fully loaded. Then, straining at their oars, the men in the boats would fight the waves till they arrived at the land.

The trucks were backed as close to the water as possible.

Several men would push the boats as far out of the water toward the trucks as they could. Then the unloading process on the backs of the men would begin.

Each sack was carried to a flatbed truck. A man stood on each truck, stacking the bags as they arrived. Here and there a few bosses were yelling at the men. The work was hard and the men, despite the coolness of the day and the stiff breeze, were sweaty with labor. They worked ceaselessly.

Where had all the trucks come from? Lydia had never seen them in town where the streets were so narrow that not even a car could pass through most of them. Were these the men from the hotel construction? Lydia watched fascinated for a long time. Then about midafternoon she decided to walk back to her room for milk and crackers and soup. Afterwards she lay down and took a nap.

When Lydia awoke, she wondered how the unloading was proceeding and, despite a misty rain, headed straight for the end of the town where the boat was. The unloading process seemed to be unchanged except for perhaps a few less men. She found a rocky place to sit part way down the hill and watched until almost dark when the men were forced to quit.

Lydia had learned there were no harbor lights, street lights, and few home lights in this area. The Dairy Queen and her aunt's villa were about the only places with light in town— apart from the resort and the elegant villas of course. In this part of the world work ceased when the natural light faded. Therefore Lydia knew that when the first light of dawn showed the men would be there working.

Lydia went back to her aunt's villa and took out paper and pencil and scribbled a few things.

At one time in her life she had wanted to be a writer. Maybe some day she would be. The bare bulb hanging over her head took on a new importance. She stared at it until it seemed to grow bigger. It was the sun burning her eyes and lighting the world. With a sigh she went over to her bed and lay face down. It was as if she was a newborn and had to put everything together again from the beginning. She had to see and explore everything she came in contact with and assign it a place in the emptiness inside. Nothing she had assumed before was left with which to carry on. It all had been destroyed. Everything had to be thought out and felt anew. And she had so little energy. It took so much to relearn about the world. Her will was constantly strained in the effort of making her cling to life and try.

Lydia went to sleep that night feeling the enormous presence of the freighter in the room. This intruder from the outside world filled the landscapes of her confines and dominated them.

In the morning the first thing Lydia thought of was the freighter. It was almost with excitement that she dressed and hurried down to see if it was still there. The activity was just as intense as yesterday. The things being unloaded were in the same kinds of brown bags. Lydia didn't know why but somehow she had expected that something different would be unloaded today. She thought she might see the sling filled with metal pots and pans like grapes clinging in clusters to their stems. Everything she had taken for granted in her part of the world seemed to be so needed here. It was hard to believe all they were bringing were the huge brown sacks that flopped over only so far as their bulging contents would allow.

Still the activities fascinated her as much as they had the day before. It had rained heavily during the night, but here and there she could see white clouds poking through the gray ones. She sat on the hill again and watched the unloading for much of the day. Her mind thought of the freighter in the endless stretch of ocean leading to civilization somewhere. Then she thought of herself. Her mind thought of happier days when her life was different.

By late afternoon there were patches of blue in the sky

and people began to appear on the streets in greater numbers. Some came to watch the great ship being unloaded. Lydia saw that it was beginning to ride higher in the water. It was amazing that these busy insectlike men had taken enough from the ship so that it rode noticeably higher.

How much did it take to lower that dirty hunk of steel and how much did it take to let it rise again? Because Lydia had faithfully watched from the beginning, she felt she knew much more than the casual observers who were now coming down the hill. She felt she was a part of the ship and its activity and somewhat resented the johnny-come-lately on-lookers.

Lydia decided to have an early supper. She went to the Dairy Queen to get one of their strange-tasting hamburgers and a soft drink. She brought them back to her place on the hill and ate her dinner while watching the unloading.

The men had been at it two days already. I wonder how long it will take, she thought. The ship seemed enormous, and the ceaseless work involved bringing in a huge amount of bags. Surely they wouldn't finish tonight. It was getting chilly and Lydia had not brought her sweater. She decided not to stay until they finished for the day. Besides, she was a little stiff from sitting so long.

Lydia went home, got under the covers and watched the neighbor's roof for the cat. But it didn't appear and the light was fading fast. At least she was sure tomorrow would be warm and sunny.

The morning was bright and clear as Lydia had imagined it. The image of the town as being cloudy, cold, and wet was still in her mind's eye. Lydia knew one or two days of sun would erase that. She could barely wait for the warm sun to work its way into her body, however. She skipped her breakfast and hurried to the hill fearful that the boat might not be there. But it was. The freighter was riding higher in the water, but the men were busy as ever. It seemed to Lydia that there were fewer men than she remembered from the day before. She sat down to watch the unloading. The trucks were backed down to the water's edge and ready. Boats were coming and going in the water.

Lydia leaned back on her hands, closed her eyes, and tipped her head back. The sun felt so good on her face. Underneath was a cold empty sadness, but the sun warmed her outside and she was content with that.

By late morning Lydia actually began to feel hot. She was also hungry. Her diet of the past weeks even left her feeling a little dizzy. She got up from her boat-watching spot and headed for the grocery store.

Although Lydia had spent endless hours already searching the shelves for names of foods she understood and products she felt she could eat, she tried again this time. Some items, like the canned milk with its red and white label, were obviously made by American companies she knew, even though the labels were printed in Spanish. However, she often didn't have the slightest idea what the other cans were unless they showed a picture of beans or something on the label. She finally settled on some chili con carne and some more crackers. She went back to her aunt's. It was the hottest part of the day now so it would be good to be inside for lunch.

After lunch, she decided to wash her hair before going back to the cliff. She then put on clean slacks and top—one of her few remaining sets. She took a pad of paper and a pencil. Maybe I'll feel like writing something, she thought. She stepped out in the afternoon sun. The buildings of the town had lost the gray look they had in the rain. Instead, they looked dirty-white again. The streets were dry and dusty. Things had returned to normal.

However, as Lydia turned the corner toward the ocean a violent emptiness greeted her eyes. The boat was gone. She stood and stared. The ocean stretched empty as far as she could see. She felt a welling sense of panic, of being abandoned.

How could it have gone? The men had been working as hard as ever just a few hours before. There was no clue that they were close to finishing. She stood feeling empty and desolate. The boat had gone. It wasn't here. It had gone. The boat's coming had had special meaning. It had been an event, something new to do. It had been all there was to do. Now, it was gone. It had sailed away leaving its own kind of oblivion.

To Lydia, her fragile contact with the wide world had disappeared. Here she was again, alone, hurt. She didn't know what to do. She stood a long while trying to deal with the shock of the boat's being gone. Finally she wandered back to her aunt's villa. She tried to think of what to do. She sat on the bed. Could she cry? I'll make myself, she thought. I can't let anymore sorrow get inside. I'll try and make myself cry. I've got to cry some more of my sadness out before anymore gets in. Soon the tears, which were falsely started, became real. Lydia sobbed for all the people who had known loss, who had mourned, who had wished that life had been different for them.

Finally Lydia lay back on the bed and dozed for awhile. A loud knocking at the door awakened her. She startled. No one had ever come to the villa since she had been there. She didn't know what to do. A sense of fear overtook her. She went to the window in front. A man stood at the door knocking. For awhile she thought of pretending she wasn't there, but she also knew that if there were some legitimate reason for his being there, she ought to find out.

Finally she went to the door timidly. "Who's there?" she asked in a soft voice.

The word the man said sounded something like "telegram."

Lydia opened the door and took the piece of paper from his hand. When he looked at her instead of going away, she realized she was probably expected to pay him something. She got her purse and put some money in his hand. His look of pleasure indicated she had probably given him too much. Never mind. She had spent hardly any money since coming here anyway.

Lydia shut the door and tore open the telegram. It read: "Lydia, your mother is in the hospital. Please come home. Will meet your plane as soon as you let us know when you are coming. Best to Aunt Milly and Uncle Ted. Jim."

Lydia walked back to the bedroom and sat on the bed. Was there a choice? Had there ever been one? She then got up and automatically began to pack.

She would be thrust back into the world, would have to go back with the pain still there and try to function, try to help if needed. She hadn't been here long enough. She wondered what the time spent here had meant, if it meant anything at all. She wondered what had happened to her mother.

Lydia pictured the scene at the American airport. Crowds of people bustling off the planes. Clumps of people waiting to meet them. Sun streaming through the airport glass windows onto the purple-blue carpet.

And there would be some of her family. "Hi," someone would say. "Did you have a good vacation?"

Lydia's eyes filled with tears. She needed to cry in private just one more time. She closed her suitcase. Home. She was going home. She didn't want to go but maybe it didn't matter. She was going.

GEORGE

George sat uncomfortably in a stuffed chair opposite the psychologist he had asked to see. He wondered why he had asked to come and even more why he had followed through and actually come. He didn't know whether his resentment at being there showed on his face but he didn't care.

A clinical or counseling psychologist is a nonmedical doctor (Ph.D. or Ed.D.) who is trained to give psychological tests and treat mental problems with various types of psychotherapy, including individual, group, and family therapies. Usually psychologists have had four years of undergraduate college, one to two years of education leading to a master's degree (M.S. or M.A.), and a doctor's degree (Ph.D., Psy.D. or Ed.D) which requires at least three more years of study in a department or school of psychology or education.

The man was acting pleasant enough. But as George looked around at the nice furnishings, he thought, "Mr. Big Bucks. Look at that nice desk. He charges people an awful lot of money."

"You don't look very happy about being here," the man began.

George wished the man had a beard like Sigmund Freud. All people who treated nuts were supposed to have beards. This man didn't. As a matter of fact, he had a rather boyish look and the fact that he wore casual clothes enhanced that look. George guessed he was in his late twenties or early thirties.

"I'm not," George replied. There was no point in beating around the bush.

The conversation seesawed back and forth for awhile. To George it seemed that everything he did to try to anger the psychologist was somehow blunted or skillfully turned aside or avoided. He just couldn't get the psychologist to meet him head on and fight about anything. At the same time, the psychologist didn't come right out and say much. George was mad because it seemed as if the psychologist was withholding something, not sharing things—like he knew something George didn't know.

On the other hand, the psychologist didn't show that in what he said. His questions were fairly straightforward. Gradually George eased up a bit and began talking about how things weren't going quite right for him. He was surprised when the hour was over. The psychologist indicated an interest in having George come back if he wanted to. George said he'd think it over. It was a lot of money to pay someone. However, George knew inside money was not the issue. George's mother said she'd find the money for him to go for awhile if he wanted, and that she would not tell his father. George knew he just had to resolve his inner battle over whether he could manage his life as well as he wanted or whether he needed some help.

To George's surprise he went back the next week. He really hated himself for doing it. On the other hand, he felt a need to go just one more time. He talked with the psychologist about the pressure he had always felt from his dad to be super-best in everything. He talked about how he resented his mother for being so humdrum—so milquetoast—for not thinking about any of the serious things that he often worried about. He talked about how he resented Geraldine for being so weird, about how he really didn't know what he wanted to do. His father had always talked to him about going to engineering school but he wasn't sure that interested him. He didn't know much about what chemical, aeronautical, or electrical engineers did. But he knew his father's firm used some of them and they made good money and that was why his dad wanted him to be one.

When the psychologist said it was time to stop, George became very angry. He resented the fact that he had talked about very personal things to the psychologist, and while he had seemed to be listening and caring about what he said, he was able just to cut it off. George was furious. "I'm just another paying sucker to him," he thought to himself and stalked out without saying goodbye.

The next week George missed his appointment and the following week when he went back, he was stoned. He loved the floaty way he handled the whole session. "I really stuck it to that guy," he later thought with glee.

But as the week wore on, the satisfaction of having seen the psychologist while on drugs quickly faded and George felt empty and depressed. With reluctance he admitted to himself it wasn't the psychologist who needed help, it was George. And his being foolish at his sessions or wasting them by not going wasn't hurting the psychologist, it was hurting him. George decided he wanted to give it one more try. He wasn't sure what he wanted out of seeing the psychologist. On the other hand, he didn't know where else to turn to figure why his life seemed to be getting worse rather than getting better.

So the next week George went back without first having used grass. He genuinely felt grateful for having someone to talk to. He particularly wanted to talk about why he had picked a fight with Marilyn just when they were getting back together again. He wanted to date her, but her telling him what to do drove him wild. Why hadn't he just put up with it like he used to? Why'd he have to explode like he did and walk out? Among other things, the psychologist said he was glad George had come to the conclusion that he was angry about a lot of things, and that the way he expressed his anger (like blowing up at Marilyn) or avoided his anger (by submerging his feelings in drug use) was creating more problems for him than it was solving.

George found it very painful when they started to talk about why he felt so angry. The memories of what George felt were his father's insensitivities or his cruelties to George when he was little brought tears to his eyes. Like the time when George was still afraid of the water and his father decided to put him in over his head to make him learn how to swim. George recalled his fear and panic and his pleading for his father's help as he kept slipping under the water. He remembered his father standing there out of reach, just watching him. When he finally struggled to the point where he could stand up, George remembered his father saying, "Well, I was right after all; you could do it." And George remembered saying nothing but feeling a deep hatred for his father for putting him in that situation and not understanding how terrified he had been, and how terrible it had been to plead for help and have his father not help him.

Reliving some of those memories brought almost more anguish than George thought he could bear. On the other hand, somehow getting them out and looking at them from a more grownup perspective was in its own strange way helpful.

Later on as George thought back to his session with the psychologist that week, he was surprised to find it was *not* the things between him and his father he talked about that he remembered most. Instead, he remembered the sense of support he got from having someone to talk to who didn't blame him for his feelings, his thoughts, what he had done, or how he was reacting now. The psychologist really seemed to be on George's side in wanting to help him gain more understanding about what made him think and feel the way he did, and then get on with his life.

A mental-health professional can often be of great help to an adolescent who is struggling with becoming independent. The professional is not likely to respond emotionally as parents would to whatever is said because his or her job is to be objective. Therefore, a young person can turn to the professional for parentlike help without worrying that the adult will try to take over and return him or her to childhood.

Moreover, the adolescent can confide secrets, talk of struggles, and express strong feelings without any fear of ridicule or retaliation. The fact that time with the mental-health professional is limited by the length of individual sessions and that the adolescent can always not come back, add to the feeling of independence.

As he got ready for bed that night, George was still thinking about that. He also wondered if those were the kinds of things that Geraldine talked about with her psychiatrist. A timid knock at the door interrupted his thinking.

"Who's there?" George asked. It wasn't as if he didn't know. His parents were out for the evening and only he and Geraldine were home.

"It's me, Geraldine," a voice replied.

"Come in," George called. He really thought it was odd that Geraldine wanted to come to his room. She hadn't even come down his hall in a year or more. They hated each other so much that it was an unwritten rule that they stayed out of each other's way as much as possible. They never went into each other's territory.

"George," Geraldine began hesitantly after she had entered the room. "I need your help."

George was surprised. One, Geraldine hadn't asked for his help in anything for about five years. Two, Geraldine had been on some sort of drug since she came home from the hospital and everyone felt she was doing much better. His parents had even felt good enough that they could now go out occasionally in the evenings without having to worry about Geraldine.

Drugs used to help emotional problems affect the symptoms but do not eliminate the causes of the problem. Therefore, many mental-health professionals would prefer not to use drugs if the emotional problem can be solved by talking about it. Complications of drugs can be avoided in this manner and the person will learn how to handle similar emotional problems in the future. On the other hand, if drug use can help with the problem, the cost of overall treatment may be reduced and the negative effects of the problem lessened. Plus, there is no assurance that truly understanding and confronting the problem will prevent the person from having other problems they can't handle. Although among mental-health professionals, psychiatrists are the only ones who can write prescriptions for drugs, psychologists, social workers, and nurses, for example, can arrange for their patients to receive drugs through a physician if the drugs are truly needed.

———————————

George noticed the distressed look on Geraldine's face. "What is it, Gerry?" he asked, and then was surprised that he had reverted to the name he had used for her when they were little.

"Thank God, I'm on that drug now, because things have cleared for me and I can see that I'm in real trouble. I don't know what would have happened if they hadn't been able to treat me. I might never have realized what's going on. As a matter of fact, we may all be in trouble. George, come down to my room while we talk about this. I don't like your room as well as mine," Geraldine suddenly said, turning and going out the door.

George got up and followed Geraldine down the hall. Since she had been on the drug, he had noticed a remarkable change in how she acted. She actually seemed normal at times or what he supposed Geraldine might be like if she were normal. In some ways, it was like having a sister for the first time in years. He wondered what it must feel like being Geraldine and being a new person for the first time in years—it must be almost like having a hole in the middle of your life. It must be as if you were a child and then you became a teenager and you missed out on all the ten- to thirteen-year-old stuff that prepared you to be a teenager.

Geraldine motioned for George to sit down on the chair next to her bed while she perched on it. "Well," she began, "at first I didn't think anything of it."

"Geraldine, what are you talking about?" George asked.

"Now I know they know who I am and they're after me."

"Geraldine, stop rambling and start making sense. I don't know what you're talking about," George repeated.

"Well, you remember the robbery of that little all-night grocery store—you know the convenience store chain they have all over the city; this one is on Maple . . ."

"Yeah," said George in a puzzled voice. "Wasn't that the one where they killed the guy at the store but there weren't any witnesses so they don't have any idea who did it?"

"Yes," said Geraldine. "That's the one." She hesitated and then went on. "But there was one witness."

"There was?" said George. "I didn't hear about that. It wasn't on television. Hey," he suddenly demanded, "how do you know there was a witness?"

"Because I was it!" Geraldine said.

George looked at her. If he hadn't known she was on the drug, he might just have gotten up and walked out, but she'd been so normal.

There are various kinds of drugs used in treating people with mental-health problems. One kind is antianxiety *drugs or minor tranquilizers. These help people feel less anxious about their problems. Among the commonly used drugs in this category are meprobamate, diazepam and chloridiaze-poxide. (Common brand names for these drugs are Miltown, Equanil, Valium, Librium). Another type of drug is* antidepressants. *These make the person feel less depressed and some have a calming effect. Among the commonly used drugs are doxepin, desipramine, amitriptcyline. (Brand names for these are Sinequan, Norpramin, Elavil, Tofranil). These have largely replaced amphetamines (Benzadrine) and dextroamphetamine (Dexadrine) which are stimulants and have little effect on depression but increase people's energy levels.*

Major tranquilizers *are generally used to treat only the most severe emotional problems. These help people who feel panic or extreme excitement, who have disturbed thinking or are overly suspicious, who experience delusions, and who are extremely withdrawn or neglectful of themselves. Among the commonly used drugs in this category are trifluoperazine, haloperidol, chlorpromazine (brand names are Stelazine, Haldol, Thorazine). Lithium carbonate (Lithane) is a drug used to treat manic-depression if the condition is not so severe that it requires a faster-acting drug.*

"C'mon. Are you kidding me?"

Geraldine looked at him very seriously. George could see she was really scared.

"No, George, it's the truth. But you're the only one I can turn to. Since I've had problems, I know no one will believe me. They'll just think it's some strange thing I dreamed up. But it's the truth. Honest, George. It's the truth but no one will believe me. You're my only hope."

George started to say something but Geraldine went on.

"George, there were two men. One wore jeans with a green T-shirt with one of those little polo ponies on it. The other one had on gray slacks and there was a rip in his back pocket where he must have taken his wallet in and out. He had on an old, red-plaid, faded long-sleeve shirt rolled up at the sleeves."

"Geraldine, how'd you happen . . ."

"See," said Geraldine, "remember that night when I had gone to Beverly's house in the evening? That was the night it happened. See, Beverly and I wanted some cheese chips but she couldn't leave because her parents were out and we were supposed to be taking care of her little sister. Anyway, I said I'd walk down to the store and I did. It turned out all their potato chips and pretzels and stuff were in the back of the store. I knelt down because the cheese chips weren't on the upper shelf and I figured they were probably on the bottom shelf. Anyway, when I was looking for them, that's when the men came in. I guess they didn't see me. Anyway, I heard what was going on so I stayed hidden."

George remembered that his mom had let Geraldine go over to Beverly's house. It was the first time she had gone over to their cousin's since she got home from the hospital. And it was just about the time of the holdup when the clerk was killed. George was puzzled. He didn't know whether or not to believe Geraldine. But how would she know such little things like torn pants pocket if she hadn't really seen it?

"Go on," George said, "what happened?"

"Well, after I heard the shots I must have panicked. I just got up and ran for the back door."

"Why didn't you stay hidden?"

"Oh, George, I should have. I know I should have." Geraldine looked frightened as she recalled her actions. "But I guess I was so upset and I thought they might decide to get other stuff in the store. So I just panicked."

"Well, did they see you?"

"Of course they saw me. I heard one of them yell 'Get her.' But remember that backyard shortcut where you cut through those people's yard that have the birdbath and switch to the upper part with the ditch and cut back down the trail next to the condominiums?"

"Yeah."

"Well, I went that way, and you know in the dark unless you really know where you are going and what you are doing, you can't possibly find the way. You just get all mixed up in the fences and bushes. So I got away pretty easily because they couldn't follow me. But George . . ." Geraldine reached out and touched his arm pleadingly. "They know who I am!"

"What makes you say that?" George felt drawn to the sincerity in Geraldine's voice. "Did they get a really good look at you?"

"Well," said Geraldine, "I didn't think so at the time. But now I know they did."

"Hey, what does Beverly say about this?" George demanded, wondering why their cousin or aunt or uncle hadn't called his mom or dad. "Why doesn't . . ."

"Oh no," said Geraldine, "I didn't want to involve her. So I just told her I was on my way to the store when I heard all these police sirens and everything. I told her that when I got there, the police had it blocked off and they wouldn't let me near the place. She had heard the sirens, so she believed me."

Geraldine was so earnest and the details seemed so real— like getting away through the cutoff they both knew—that George began to take Geraldine seriously. She looked so beseeching now. George recalled in an unexpected flash how he had told the psychologist of his own pleading with his father when he was drowning in the water and how his father had ignored him and what that had done to him. He didn't want that to happen to Geraldine.

"What do you mean, they know who you are?" George asked.

"They do," said Geraldine. "And they're trying to get to me. They know I can identify them." Geraldine hesitated, then went on. "Well, you know the phone calls we started having . . ."

George had picked up the phone and found no one there

often enough over the past month to know what Geraldine meant. But also George thought he could hear some kids laughing a couple of times. "Geraldine, no. Those are just kids playing jokes. I used to do that when I was in fourth grade too."

"No," Geraldine said strongly. "That's them—the murderers trying to get me when I'm home alone. And then you know our mailbox was knocked down . . ."

"Yeah, some kids probably did that with their car and I bet I know who, too," George added. It was customary for high-school seniors to take out a mailbox or two in celebration of their graduation. It happened every year and George bet he knew who had picked theirs. The captain of the basketball team had never quite forgiven George for getting grounded during that crucial next-to-last game when they thought they had a chance for the championship.

"No," said Geraldine firmly. "It was the murderers. Because now you know the mailman can't leave the mail in the box in the street so he has to come up to the house. Last week . . ."

"Geraldine, I don't know," George said hesitantly.

"George, listen," Geraldine pleaded. "When I was home alone last Tuesday, a man came to our door wearing a mailman's uniform but he wasn't our regular mailman. He stood there ringing the bell and then he tried the door knob. I watched him from the upstairs window. And when the door didn't open, I saw him take something from his pocket and start fiddling with the key hole."

"He was really trying to get into the house?" George asked in wonderment.

"Yes," said Geraldine. "I could tell he was and he might have made it too, only Mrs. Phillips pulled into her drive across the street and he just left."

"But maybe he just wanted to set the mail inside the screen

door and you thought he was fiddling with the inside lock."

"But," said Geraldine, "he didn't leave *any* mail at all! I checked!"

George was startled. A mailman who tried hard to get in the door with no mail. Although it was hard to believe, if these things were really going on and Geraldine was right, she might really be in danger. And true, she was the perfect one to have these things happen to and to have the murderers get away with it. She couldn't turn to anyone and have them believe her because people didn't know yet that the drugs were really helping her.

Momentarily Geraldine acted as if she was going to be overwhelmed by her fears, but then she pulled herself together and went on. "And remember last week when that strange dog came up our drive just as dad was about to get the newspaper and the dog carried it off. There must be some scheme to have an excuse for a fake delivery boy to start coming up to our house, maybe even try to get in with the paper."

George had thought it strange that a black dog had just run up, got their newspaper, and took off with it. However George loved it. He thought it was hysterical, particularly the part where his dad was running after the dog and one of his slippers came off and he kept right on going until he stepped on a bee in the neighbor's yard.

"George," Geraldine reached out and touched his arm. "And I think they're after you too, George."

"What do you mean?" George asked. "Why me?"

"Because they probably figure I told you what the men looked like so they think you can identify them too. That's why I decided to tell you. It wasn't fair for you to be in danger and not know about it."

George tried to put everything together, the strange phone calls, the knocked-over mailbox, the paper being snatched. It really seemed as if something was happening. George paused.

"Look, Geraldine, if this is really going on, we ought to go to the police."

"No," Geraldine said quickly. "I'm sure there's someone at the police who's protecting them."

"Geraldine, how do you know that?" George struggled to grasp what she was saying.

"They think I can't understand them when they change and talk, but I can."

"What do you mean?" George felt really confused now.

"I see them in the trees outside the window and I know they're watching and I've even sneaked up in the attic and looked down on them and listened to them. And they say they're going to kill me." The terror in her voice had increased. "Oh George, what am I going to do?" She flung herself in George's arms.

"There, there, Gerry, what do you mean . . . in the trees?" George asked, pushing her away just enough to see her face.

" 'Cause they can change," Geraldine said and her eyes narrowed. "They can turn into squirrels and climb trees." She flung her head against George's chest again and began sobbing. "They can change into any animal. That dog that stole the paper. That wasn't a real dog. That was them."

Geraldine hugged George close. "And the dog that ran in front of your car that time so you had an accident. That was one of them too."

George started to say something. And then suddenly he remembered the robbery had not been at the Maple Street store but at another convenience store that was across town from his cousin's.

———————

Some people who are schizophrenic may sound and act quite reasonable. Yet they may believe that everyone else is against them, that others are trying to do strange things to them such as putting spells on them or trying to destroy them using mysterious forces. They may commit criminal acts in trying to "get back at" those who they think are going to harm them.

Geraldine sobbed, "Oh George, I'm so scared." She was trembling all over.

George looked up and his glance fell on the night table next to Geraldine's bed. There on the table sat an unopened bottle of pills. George remembered the bottle because he was with his mother when she picked up the refill last week. So Geraldine had not been taking the drug she needed. And then he remembered his father arguing with his mother because she had gotten home late, having stopped at the drugstore. And George remembered his father saying, "Well, damn, she's well enough to get her own pills and take her own pills too for that matter. You've got to stop coddling her, Mildred. All this stuff is making a weakling out of her. She's got to learn to stand on her own two feet and take care of herself."

George winced. So his mom must have stopped reminding Geraldine to take her pills. And Geraldine really wasn't well enough to take that kind of control of her life.

People generally find it not to be a problem to take minor tranquilizers and antidepressant drugs, although all drugs may have some side effects. People who take major tranquilizers, however, often have a real dislike of them and have to struggle against not taking the drug when they should. Patients who have stopped taking major tranquilizers constitute a high proportion of the people who are readmitted to hospitals for conditions similar to those for which they were first admitted. The beneficial effects of major tranquilizers can last for days or weeks after they are stopped. However, a stressful event can cause the major emotional problem for which the drug was taken to return.

"George, please help me." Geraldine's voice seemed small and helpless.

"There, there," George said, tears coming to his eyes. "There, there, Geraldine. Everything's going to be all right. I'll take care of you. I'll take care of you."

And then for the first time in a long time, George was able to remember a time when he had liked Geraldine. He remembered when they were much younger and had had endless hours of fun playing hide and seek together. He remembered times when his dad had come down hard on him, and Geraldine, as little as she was then, had stuck up for him to the point of being punished herself. He remembered when Geraldine had been a laughing child who liked to tease him in fun. And then he remembered how Geraldine had grown very serious and very quiet. How Geraldine had stopped having friends. And George hadn't been her friend either. He was too busy with his own life, his own things. He had just stopped being involved with her.

George felt how scared and helpless Geraldine was, clinging to him.

His eyes began to water. How selfish and self-centered he had been. Geraldine had probably needed him, needed at least one person to stand up for her, to be her friend. And he hadn't been that when he could have been. My God, who else did she have. His father only saw things his way. His mother wouldn't have been able to be a friend even if she had seen it was needed. He saw it but didn't know what was happening.

"Oh, Gerry," George hugged her. "Oh, Gerry, I'm so sorry. I'm so sorry." The tears fell freely down his face.

7

What If It Gets Better Instead of Worse?

MARTIN

"Martin, Martin!" A voice called from behind him as he was going out the front door of the school.

Martin slowed down and turned to see who it was. The bright fall sunlight made him squint. He could hardly believe that the summer was over and he was back in school already.

Martin had had the best summer ever. Usually his summers were spent behind the counters of one of the local fast food restaurants amid the smell of french fries and hamburgers.

This summer had been different. His mental-health worker had convinced a local computer company to take Martin on at a minimum wage to learn about computers and simple programming. The worker was convinced that with Martin's analytical mind and creativity, he had potential for something like computers. He also was convinced Martin needed an outlet for his energy and talents.

Martin had taken to computers immediately. He was at work before anyone else and stayed late when he could. He took computer manuals home with him at night and studied them. By the end of the first two weeks, he had learned all the company had thought they might teach him in the entire summer. From then things just took off. His boss liked him because he was quiet and enthusiastic. He was also a dedicated worker. His boss began giving him more and more complicated things to do. By the end of the summer, his boss was talking about his working during vacations in the school year and coming back the next summer to do advanced computer work. Martin was ecstatic.

"Martin!" The girl who had been calling him caught up with him. "Martin," she smiled her best smile, "could you set me up on your computer thing tomorrow? Please?"

Martin looked at her. It was Sarah, a new cheerleader. She had dark, pretty curly hair and sparkly eyes. She might even be as pretty as Jennie Brock.

"Well," Martin hesitated. "To be honest, I've already had three kids sign up for tomorrow after school, and that's about all I can handle and get home on time. I could maybe do it Monday."

"Oh, Martin," Sarah said. "I really wanted to use it this week. Isn't there any way? Please? I'm a real quick learner," she added.

Martin looked at her. Actually she did look smart. He bet she did learn fast. Someone had even said she was a straight-A student. That was kinda unusual for a cheerleader. Not that cheerleaders were dumb. Most of them were B students. It was just rare to get one who got straight As.

"Okay," Martin said and chuckled to himself. Despite a summer of group therapy he guessed he was still a sucker for pretty girls who wanted him to help them. "I guess I can come to school early tomorrow if you can. Why don't you meet me at seven and I can get you coded in and show you how to use it before school starts. Then later on next week if you are having any problems, we can schedule some time again."

"Thanks," said Sarah with genuine feeling. "Everyone said you were very nice and I guess they were right. Bye now."

Martin watched her skip down the steps. Her skirt made a fascinating swinging motion as she went. He nodded to himself. Yes, she sure was pretty.

"Hey, Martin," a hand clapped him on the shoulder.

Martin turned and saw Luiz Bandura grinning at him.

"Martin, I showed the coach my printout and he couldn't fight it. He said he guessed as long as I did what it said, he wouldn't stop me. Man, this is the greatest invention since the time machine."

Martin smiled. "Yeah," he said, "but no one's invented the time machine yet."

"Oh yeah, you're right," said Luiz. "I guess I saw that in a movie this weekend. Anyway, thanks. This is the greatest thing to hit football training since . . . hmmmm . . . well, since Gatorade."

Martin sighed. He wasn't sure he liked his new computer program compared with gatorade. On the other hand, people saw it the way they wanted to.

"Okay, Luiz, see you." Martin started on down the school steps himself. Near the bottom he stopped to check to make sure he'd remembered his English book. He found he had.

"Martin!" Another voice, a more grownup one, called to him.

Martin stopped while the principal caught up with him.

"Miss Blakely, the cafeteria manager, tells me if many more kids get into your program, she's going to have to adopt a whole new style of ordering food," the principal said with a smile on his face.

"Gee, I'm sorry, sir," Martin said. "I really didn't mean to cause the cafeteria any problems." That was the trouble, Martin thought, whenever you did one thing, it always affected another. For example, when he set the fire in the school basement to get the money for Jennie's shoes, it had disrupted classes all day and he hadn't meant to do that. The thought of his taking the money made him wince a little. Even though he had anonymously mailed the money back to Miss Blakely out of his first paycheck last summer, he still felt guilty for having taken it in the first place.

"Don't worry about it, Martin," the principal went on. "Miss Blakely and I agreed that having this many kids all of a sudden interested in nutrition was probably worth any changes in ordering that she'll have to do. You know, Martin, it really is a very clever idea you've got there. I'm not sure you could exactly call it a science project, but you might try entering it in one of those state science competitions. I'm not sure it would win anything, but it might just spur some interest. And you know companies often go to those science fairs to scout for people they might like to hire in the future. Think about it." The principal patted Martin on his shoulder and went on his way.

Martin stood thinking. His idea had really been very simple after all. All the kids in his school liked junk food. He didn't know of anyone who didn't. Even he liked it. But everyone was always harping on kids about their diets and their poor nutrition.

Actually, he sorta got the idea from one of the kids in the therapy group whose mother was always after her about her diet. He paused. He no longer went to the group therapy. Both he and his mental-health worker thought he no longer needed it. Still he wondered how some of the kids were doing. In a way, he missed having them to share with.

Anyway, since he was working with computers, he wondered why he couldn't write a program that would help kids know after they had eaten their junk food (which had to have some nutrition in it) just how much of something else that was nutritious they would have to eat to have a good diet. So he had set out to do it in late summer and had been able to finish it up on the school computer. Now any kid who wanted could plug in basic information about himself or herself—body type: big bones, medium bones, small bones; height, sex, current weight, desired caloric intake (in case they either wanted to lose weight or gain weight). After plugging in information about himself or herself, a kid could plug in acceptable foods—first a list of the junk foods they liked, and then a list of the good stuff they could tolerate, like carrots, lettuce, orange juice, liver, etc. If they really detested something they didn't put it on the list.

Martin smiled to himself. It really had taken quite a bit of research on food to get the system right, but now that it was all programmed in it was working perfectly.

Anyway, the kids could use the system in two ways. One, the kids could plug in what they knew they wanted to eat the next day, like pancakes, hamburger and fries, coke, potato chips and a hotdog. Then the kids could ask the computer what else they needed to add to have a balanced diet. The computer would search the food lists. For example, Martin had learned bananas were very nutritious—eleven essential vitamins and minerals—so the computer might add a banana-split ice-cream sundae. Of course, if a kid was watching his or her weight, the computer might just list banana. The computer also told the proportion—like half a banana, or a quarter of a carrot, or four ounces of orange juice—so a kid could get away with eating as little as possible the things he or she didn't like. The computer always tried to add junk food first to balance the diet.

The second way a kid could use the system was to plug in at the end of the day what he or she had already had to eat for breakfast and lunch, to find out what he or she should have for dinner.

Martin smiled. It was surprising how many kids wanted to list pizza as junk food when it was really very nutritious. So they really were learning something about nutrition just as he had in doing the program.

Martin's own popularity had zoomed. He wasn't a popular kid in the regular sense—one who got invited to all the parties. He was popular in the sense that kids were interested in what he had come up with and liked to talk to him. He could tell they had also developed some new respect for him.

Martin looked both ways and then crossed the street. An image flashed in his mind just as he reached the other side. For a long time he had been a little kid, and when he had given that up he had been in a no man's land, not grownup yet but not a little kid either. The only ties he had were to the past, yet there was no going back. It was like being in the middle of the street and knowing you had to get out of being there, knowing you had to get to the other side. But since you hadn't been to the other side, you had no ties to it, no memories of it, and no idea what it would be like.

Then somehow one day you were there. You'd made it. You were on the other side. Martin thought about how he was looking forward to this, his senior year in school, and to working at the computer company on vacations and during next summer, and if he were lucky, going on in computers either in a college or a training school. He realized that for the first time he had some ties to the future. Maybe that was what growing up was all about: having more ties to the future than you had with the past. He didn't know, but it felt good.

LYDIA

The third-period bell rang. Lydia gathered up her books and headed for her locker. Next period was lunch and she was very hungry. Cecilia had promised to meet her at the side door and, since it was such a nice day, sit under the trees and have lunch with her. She put the books from her morning classes down so she could work the combination on her lock.

"Lydia," a hesitant voice called from behind her.

Lydia turned to see Neil Fragonard standing behind her. Neil was in the same grade as Lydia and they had English together.

"Hi, Neil," Lydia responded, wondering why he had stopped to talk with her.

"Look," Neil said. "My family owns a boat and we're going sailing this weekend. I was wondering if you'd like to come along this Saturday. The boat's up at Lake Buford."

Lydia was surprised. She wondered why he was asking her. "Gee, thanks, Neil," she said. "But my mom's been ill so I promised my father I'd take care of the kids Saturday afternoon. Then Cecilia was going to help me study social studies Saturday night. I missed a lot last month when I was away. But thanks a lot for asking, that's really nice of you."

Neil looked disappointed and started to turn away. Then he brightened and turned back. "Well, maybe you'd just like to come for the sail in the morning."

"But wouldn't that mess up your plans? I mean, not having someone who could come all day?"

"No, I'd rather have you come for half a day," Neil said warmly.

Lydia hesitated. Then she thought. Why not? She really hadn't done hardly anything since she'd been back. "Well, okay then," Lydia said. "I'll have to check with my dad to make sure he agrees." Then she caught herself. *Dad,* she had called Jim, *Dad.*

"Great," Neil was saying. "I'll talk with you in English tomorrow and then we can arrange a time for me to pick you up." He turned and strode off down the hall.

Lydia looked after him. What in the world could have made him ask her? Then she remembered the paper she had written for English. She had written about the ship she had seen unloading at the village, except she had included a little boy. The story was about the little boy's love for the big boat that came twice a year to his town and . . . Of course, that was it! The teacher had liked her story so much she had had Lydia read it out loud in class. It probably made Neil think she liked boats.

Lydia took her lunch down from her locker, shut the door, and locked it. This would be her first date since she had come back. Actually, it would be her first date since she had broken up with Wayne. She sighed. The thought of Wayne still hurt, but perhaps not in quite the same way. Besides, Neil was a nice person. He studied hard and was assistant editor of the school paper. It would be nice to go sailing with him.

Cecilia was waiting for her at the side door as she had promised. As they went outside, Cecilia noticed the puzzled expression on Lydia's face.

"Hey, what's up?" Cecilia asked.

"The weirdest thing just happened," Lydia said. "I was talking to Neil Fragonard and . . ."

"What's so weird about talking with Neil Fragonard?" Cecilia interrupted.

"And I told him before I could go sailing, I'd have to ask my *Dad*." Lydia turned to Cecilia. "*Dad*. I called Jim, *Dad*. I've never done that before in my life. I don't really think of him as my dad. I think of him as mom's new husband, and Marcia's father."

"That *is* weird," Cecilia said.

"But so many funny things have happened since I've been back," Lydia went on. "You know with my mother having been so ill and no one except me to care for Finney and Marcia after school till Jim gets home from work, it's made me feel much more a part of my family. I mean they really needed me to come back and when I got back, everyone was depending on me."

Cecilia and Lydia sat down under a tree on the school grounds. Lydia unwrapped her sandwich but didn't begin to eat.

"It's funny, too, how I've begun to feel differently about mom too. You know, she's always been so perfect—you know, in charge of her life, in charge of her career, in charge of us, the kids. Somehow when she got sick and couldn't take charge of anything, I saw her differently. And when for awhile I thought she might even die, it made me realize how much more important she was to me than I thought. It was okay before that to reject her and to want to run away from her. But that was sorta because she was always going to be there." Lydia paused. "Am I making any sense?" Without waiting for an answer, she went on, "I really do love her, you know. We have our problems but I love her."

Cecilia didn't reply. She just listened thoughtfully to her friend.

Lydia began again. "One other interesting thing is that my mom said, in a different way, it made me much more important to her too. She says I'm the only daughter she will ever give birth to and that I was her firstborn. Because of that, I have a specialness to her that no one else can have. Thinking she was going to die and maybe not see me grow up made her think all the more about how special I was to her."

Adolescents gain a great deal of support from peers who are understanding even when their relationships are mainly a sharing of confusion. Although peer relationships lack many of the constructive problem-solving elements of mental-health counseling from a professional, they have value in that they allow the adolescent to face and think about his or her problems.

"Does your mom know yet you went out of the country alone?" Cecilia asked, changing the subject slightly.

"No. Actually, Jim only found out a couple of weeks ago. I guess when Aunt Milly called to find out how mom was doing, she said she hoped she would be better by summer so I wouldn't miss my trip with them. That blew that!"

"What'd Jim say when he found out?"

"Well, it was kinda funny," Lydia said. "He just came up to me and said he had found out I'd been down in my aunt's villa all by myself. Then he said he was glad I came back, and he just hugged me. You know, he's been under a lot of strain from nearly losing mom." Lydia hesitated, then added, "As I said, it's weird. Everything seems so different now. But then again, perhaps a lot of it has always been that way. Maybe it's just me that's different."

Cecilia reached over and touched Lydia's hand. "You must have been feeling very lonely down at your aunt's all by yourself."

"Yes." In a flash all the feelings came back to Lydia. "I was lonely and hurting and really wanted to die. But I guess I either didn't have the courage to kill myself, or else I just had too strong a will to live in spite of all the hopeless feelings I had."

"You know," Cecilia said, "After you told me about your trip and how you felt so awful when you went away, I talked to my social worker about you."

Most social workers who perform mental-health services complete four years of undergraduate college and a two-year graduate program with specialization in mental health leading to a master's degree (M.S.W. or M.S.S.W.) Some social workers may go on for three or more years of additional training leading to a Ph.D. or D.S.W. Social workers engage in individual, group, or family therapy. Other professionals who perform mental-health services are nurses, occupational therapists, paraprofessionals (such as mental-health workers, mental-health assistants), psychiatric counselors, activity therapists, rehabilitation counselors, and pastoral counselors.

"Hmmm," said Lydia taking a bite of her sandwich at last.

"Yes," Cecilia said. "I hope you don't mind."

"Nmnuo," said Lydia through the peanut butter.

"And I told her how you seemed much more together now than just about the whole time I've known you."

Lydia thought a minute and nodded slowly in agreement.

"And my social worker said that you must have worked through a lot while you were gone and maybe even since you've come back."

"What's 'worked through'?" asked Lydia.

"Oh, it's what social workers say when they mean that you've thought a lot about things that have happened to you, and how you feel about them, and somehow adjusted to them in a way that they don't bother you or cause you to do things you don't want to do."

Lydia reflected on that a minute. "I don't know," she answered. "But somehow I do feel differently about a lot of things. I'm just not sure why. Did your social worker say anything else?"

"Well, she said it sounded like you had gone through a lot of pain and suffering and she wished you could have talked to her, or someone like her—I guess she meant someone who was trained to listen to people and help them with their problems."

"Why?"

"Because she said that maybe you could have cut short some of the stuff you went through. You know, understand better what was going on, and why you felt the way you did, and maybe even come up with better ways of reacting to it all."

Sometimes in order to find an independent role and become more adultlike, adolescents go beyond their capacity, or at least feel as if they had. When this happens, adolescents might need and want a temporary period in which they can become dependent upon someone while they regroup their sense of self and energy. At such times, adolescents need a parent or someone they can treat as a parent. Parents are often confused by this independence/dependence flux in adolescents, and do not know what is expected of them at any given time. Sometimes it is easier for adolescents who have taken a strong stance toward independence to use a mental-health professional as a parent substitute upon whom to become dependent. That way they don't lose face by returning to a childhood state with their parents. In this situation, they may seek the temporary support in decision-making they need and may then rather quickly venture out on their own again.

"Does she help you do that?" Lydia asked.

"Well, you know my life has been a royal mess. My father ran off with some woman. And my mother just seems to get attached to any guy who will give her attention. She's drinking again. And I've got to worry when and if she's coming home and who she's coming home with. Or if she doesn't come home, who's going to feed my brothers and sisters. And if I decide to feed them, if there's even anything in the house to fix."

Cecilia paused. "Yeah, I think she's a help, that is, if anyone can be a help. I'd really like someone just to play God and fix everything. But at least she's helped me sort of think through what my life is about and where it's going. Yeah, she really helps me."

"Didn't it ever bother you seeing her? I mean didn't you ever feel you were crazy or nuts or something?"

"No."

"Well, didn't you feel you weren't very grownup if you couldn't handle your own problems?"

"Well, no, because I know I'm not insane or anything, and

I don't think handling your own problems really has to do with being grownup. I mean it sorta does. But I think being able to ask for help when you need it is probably being more grownup. Anyway, before I started to see my social worker, I was really depressed. I just didn't think I could go on. I just couldn't seem to get up any energy for anything. As a matter of fact, before I started seeing her I tried to commit suicide. Did I ever tell you that?"

Lydia shook her head no. Then she added, "I guess I wasn't much of a friend to you. I mean you were always trying to be my friend and help me. And I was so concerned about myself, I guess I didn't see maybe you needed a friend too."

"Why were you so persistent about me?" Lydia suddenly asked. "I mean you were always trying to be friendly even when I snubbed you or didn't seem to care about getting to know you better."

"Well," said Cecilia, "maybe it was because when I saw you suffering, I knew some of what you must be going through. I had my social worker to talk to and it didn't look like you had anyone." Then she added laughingly, "Boy, though, you sure were determined not to let me, or anyone I guess, but Wayne, get close to you."

Lydia smiled back. She continued more seriously, "That was why Wayne was so important to me. He was the first person of the opposite sex, maybe anyone really, that I let to get to know me well. And of course with him came all the phony friends I wanted. When Wayne rejected me, I felt the worst I think anyone could possibly feel. I can't imagine any physical pain worse than the kind of pain I felt then."

"But even before that," Cecilia said, "you always seemed so troubled. Like there was always something bothering you. It was like that took all your energy so you didn't have much left to care about anyone but yourself."

"Yes," Lydia said. "I guess I haven't felt very good

about myself for a long time. I don't know why. Now though, I feel like things are changing for me. At least I hope they are. I don't ever want to go back the way I came." For an instant Lydia remembered the long tortuous walk to and from the beach. She focused again on Cecilia.

"Do you think if I ever wanted to talk to your social worker, she'd see me?"

"Sure," Cecilia said. "That's what she told me. She wished you'd had someone to talk to, and I'm sure she'd be glad to see you any time. Want me to ask her if she's got time this week?"

"No, no thanks," Lydia said assuredly. "I really don't think I need to talk to her right now. Actually just talking to you these last couple of weeks has been wonderful. No, I think I'm doing okay now. I just wanted to know in case something changes."

Some adolescents make the decision themselves that they could benefit from mental-health services. This is a sign of genuine strength and maturity on the part of the adolescent, and adults should recognize it as such. They should support this desire for help to the fullest.

Some teens who do not wish to obtain professional help think it means they are "crazy" if they go to a mental-health professional. Others see being forced to see a mental-health professional as punishment. Convincing teenagers who have difficulty recognizing they could benefit from professional help can be difficult for parents, teachers, and others. However, if it is clear that such an intervention could affect the adolescent's life course in a positive manner, then those trying to help a reluctant teen should not allow themselves to become easily discouraged and should attempt to use all their skills and resources to obtain help for him or her.

For both the teen who wants to seek help and the teen who is resistant, it is vital to be selective about the mental-health professional he or she is to be served by. If the teen first sees a person who is not skilled at working with adolescents, it may turn him or her off from seeking any further help. The age of the mental-health professional is not important, but his or her skill in relating to adolescents is crucial. Pediatricians, school personnel, people who work in the mental-health field are good resources for recommendations about therapists who have a reputation for working well with adolescents.

"Well, anytime," said Cecilia. "Just let me know."

The two friends fell silent.

Suddenly Cecilia asked, "Say, when you first told me about calling Jim, 'Dad,' about twenty minutes ago, didn't you say you told Neil Fragonard you'd go sailing with him?"

Lydia nodded and took a final bite of her sandwich.

"Say, this isn't going to turn out like the last time, is it?" Cecilia asked.

"What do you mean?" Lydia inquired.

"Well, when you started going with Wayne, you dropped most of the people who liked you, like me, and just started acting so snooty."

"Did I really do that?" Lydia asked. Then without waiting for an answer she said, "Yeah, I guess I did."

"Yep, you did," said Cecilia emphatically.

"Well, then, I tell you what." Lydia said. "If you ever see me doing that again, you just give me a card."

"A card? What . . ." Cecilia was puzzled.

"And on the card you say, 'You have an appointment with my social worker at 2 o'clock next Friday because you *really are nuts* and *really need help!*'"

Cecilia laughed. "It's a deal," she said. "It's a deal."

GEORGE

George walked out of the psychologist's office. He noted the trees already were starting to look a little bare; it was an early fall this year. That had been his last appointment with the psychologist unless he felt he needed to come back. Both the psychologist and George had agreed he'd come a long way in the few months they had been seeing each other. George saw the psychologist weekly. Particularly after his episode with Geraldine, George had felt he really needed someone outside his parents to try to help him understand things.

Secretly George had worried that he might go off the deep end like Geraldine—that it might be something hereditary in his family and he too would eventually be unstable.

Generally the mental-health professional and the person seeking help work out goals for treatment—both long- and short-range. A rough timetable can be set. Two or three sessions may achieve some specific goals. Sometimes that is all that is needed, although several months or even years are not unusual in achieving long-range goals.

Over the summer George continued to be surprised that seeing a psychologist was not at all what he had expected it to be. You didn't have to be nuts to see one. You didn't even have to have problems, truth to tell. The psychologist explained that some people came even when they felt they had no problem, simply because they wanted to help themselves become more of whoever they could be. That was still a little hard for George to understand. But then he had enough trouble making sense out of his own world without trying to understand everyone else's.

George was impressed that when he went to talk to his psychologist he didn't feel like a crazy person. It surprised him he could continue to go and not perceive himself as someone who was sick. Maybe he decided that was because some people, like Geraldine, really were sicker, which made everyone feel that if you saw someone you really had to be ready for the crazy house.

George had come to think of his psychologist as a friend. But there was a difference. The psychologist's job was to be objective, George knew, and friends didn't have to be that way. That, however, didn't stop him from being a friendly, supportive person. George saw him as special and knew by the fall that they had shared more about George's past than George might ever choose to share with anyone again in his life.

In most of the sessions the psychologist let George raise issues and examine problems. At times he asked him questions that somehow made it either easier to think about things or let him think about things in different ways.

That is not to say that George ever thought examining some of his thoughts and feelings was an easy thing to do. When he thought about many of the things that had caused him to store up so much anger, it actually hurt. But it became more bearable when George began to feel some of the anger leave him. Some came out in the sessions. Sometimes he raged at people in his life, sometimes at himself, and sometimes even at the psychologist. But he was surprised when he began to feel some of the anger inside melting away, as if it did not have to come out at all. George felt the time he and the psychologist spent talking about what made George so angry at the time, the pressures he was under, and his struggles with his parents, was probably the most helpful. He also talked about how he felt about friends, about girls, and what some of his fantasies were.

Often a very difficult task for adolescents is to distinguish between which restrictions imposed upon them by the adult world prevent their development as individuals and as adults, and which do not. In particular, it may be difficult for young people to determine which of the limits imposed by their parents are hindering their growth and development and which are basically sound guidelines that will allow them to mature within appropriate boundaries. A mental-health professional can often perform a very helpful role in this regard. He or she can help adolescents gain a firmer sense of where they are as persons and aid them in evaluating authority in their life and its impact upon them.

George smelled his mother's chicken curry the minute he opened the door. "Mom, I'm home," he called. "Do you need me to do anything? Otherwise, I'm going to do my homework." His mother never wanted him to do anything, but George had resolved to ask because it made them both feel better. There was at least some connection between them when he came home. He had wondered if his mother's pestering him about decisions had been, in part, because she really didn't know what to talk to him about. They were so different. He was interested in serious things, while she was not. She didn't really know anything about sports. A lot of contemporary morals and attitudes expressed by his friends were so different from her own she couldn't relate to them. And now that he was no longer her "little boy" who needed caring for, she really had very little in common with him.

George really couldn't say that understanding some things about his mother made him like her any better. However, he recognized she wasn't going to change. That was the way she was and would probably continue to be. And she was the only mother he was ever going to have, so he might just learn to live with her for the few more years he'd be at home. Plus he learned he didn't know everything about her. He was very surprised when his father finally found out he had been seeing the psychologist, and his mother had not let his father argue about it. She really could occasionally connect with some kind of reality and do okay by it.

"No, thanks, dear," his mother called. "You just go on and do your homework."

George hurried back to his room. This school year was really going to count toward college. And since he had goofed off so badly at the end of last year, his grade average was down. However, if he could pull off a really super senior year, and get good scores on the college entrance exams, then he might still have a chance to end up at some decent college.

He wasn't quite finished with his homework when his mother called him for dinner, but he had done most of it. He approached the dining room slowly. It was still odd to walk in and see the table set for three. Geraldine had been gone for two months now. The doctor had felt that some other setting might be better for her for awhile. A sort of halfway house. Not in the hospital but not quite in a home either. The doctor had not made any promise, but was talking about the fact that Geraldine might come home for a trial stay around Thanksgiving.

Halfway houses provide services not quite as intense as those offered in a hospital setting but more than those obtainable by patients who live at home. Halfway houses for adolescents may have eight to twenty young people who live there anytime from three months to one or two years. Young people get social and psychological support in a halfway house. Most often such a residence is used as part of a followup after-hospital treatment.

———————

George had talked with his psychologist many times about Geraldine. His psychologist said he couldn't say anything firm about her case because he was not the one who was treating her. However, he was optimistic she could be helped, although chances were she wouldn't ever be quite as fine as everyone would like her to be. She might always need her drugs.

George's father emerged from the bathroom and followed him down the hall. "Well, how did the day go, son?"

"Fine, Dad," George replied.

"How did the advanced calculus go? Giving you any trouble?"

"I dropped it, dad," George replied. They entered the dining room.

"You dropped it, dad," George's father repeated in a loud astounded voice. "I thought you were going to be an engineer. How can you do that without advanced calculus?"

"Well, dad, when I saw what was involved, I talked it over with the teacher and decided not to take it. It's very complex and it would put a lot of pressure on me to handle it. I don't need the credit for graduation and I already have a pretty good background in math. And I really need to see my grades go up."

George's father cut in, "But I told you engineers need that and if you're going to be an engineer, I want you to be a good one, one of the best. I've even got a spot picked out for you when you graduate."

"Well, dad," George began as they sat down at the table. "I like the idea of being an engineer, but I also like the idea of being a lawyer, and I like the idea of getting into computers. There are so many things that appeal to me. I've got this year of high school to think more about them. And then there's college."

"For God's sake, you just don't go to college. You go to learn something. You have to know what you want to be when you go."

"Well, dad, I bet I'll have a better idea at the end of this year. June is a long way off."

"Well," his father grumbled and pushed some mashed potatoes onto his plate before passing the bowl to George. "What do you . . . ."

"Dear, I have some news about Geraldine," his mother interrupted.

"What's that?" his father said.

"I went out to see her today and they said they were even more sure she might be able to come home at Thanksgiving. Wouldn't that be good?"

George saw the pain on his father's face. "Yes, it would be good."

George thought how funny it was that people could love someone and yet not be able to relate to them at all.

"What did Geraldine feel like? What did she say, mom?" George asked.

"Well," said his mother. "She really didn't say all that much, but she looked much brighter than when I saw her last time, like there was a little more sparkle in her eyes or something. Yes, that's what I noticed. A little more sparkle in her eyes."

George looked at his mother. The strain of the last year had been hard on her. She looked a lot older. On the other hand, there was still something very soft and pretty about her.

"Well, George," his father said, turning his attention back to him. "Any good prospects for the basketball team this year? With that center and your *star forward* graduating, you're going to be hard put to take the championship this year unless someone really improves or you get some new stars coming along."

"Well," George replied. "There's a transfer student—some guy moved here from South Carolina and they say he's pretty good. They might even let him play my position."

"Well, then what will you play? Defense?"

"No, I told the coach I'm not playing this year. I figured it was best not to wait but let him know right away."

George's father's fork hit his plate noisily. "You're not playing!" he said. "Of course you're playing. Any son of mine who's as good in sports as you are would be a fool not to play."

George saw his mother's mouth open as if to speak, but then she looked somewhat nervously at his father and closed it without saying anything.

George's father went on. "Sports makes you competitive, gives you that drive to win that you need, helps prepare you. The thrill of the game . . . I've never forgotten my senior game when we were two points ahead with one minute to go and we would be county champions. The way we dug in and kept those guys from scoring . . . God, that was a game I'll never forget. This year will be your best year, you wait and see."

"Dad, I'm not going to be playing."

"George, I want you to play and you're going to play," his dad said.

"I'm sorry, dad, I know how important sports are to you and how much you want to see me be a success at sports too. It was an awful decision for me to have to make and I admit I'm really going to miss it."

"Well, then, why the hell aren't you playing?"

"Because, dad, I've got to make good grades. I'm not going to go on and become a pro in sports, and if I study as hard as I need to and try to do sports too, I won't have any time to spend with my friends without being pressured beyond what I can handle."

"Who the hell cares if you're with your friends. Twenty years from now you may not even be living in this town and you may not know a single one of them."

"But, don't you see? I just don't want all the pressure this year. There's going to be pressure in college, I know, and I just want to do as well as I can this year so I'll be ready for it."

"It's that fool psychologist, isn't it?" His dad's voice was louder now. "He's the one that'd been telling you all that stuff."

A skilled mental-health professional has the double job of earning and keeping the trust of both the teenager and his or her parents. This can be an especially difficult task if the teenager and the parents are having problems living together and getting along with each other. Sometimes the teenager seems to relate so well to his or her therapist that the parents fear the therapist is taking over their role, and as a result the teenager will be less willing to respect and obey them. Sometimes it is necessary for the therapist to see the parents alone, or more commonly to see the parents and the teenager together, to insure the parents do not act in ways destructive to the goals of the therapy but are instead helpful and supportive of the teenager as he or she tries to work out problems.

"No, dad, he hasn't been telling me anything. I decided myself."

"I don't believe you. Since you've been seeing that shrink, you just aren't the same. How much longer is that going to go on anyway?"

George said, "I'm not going any more unless I feel I just need to check back."

"Well, that's good," said George's father. "Because maybe now you'll get some sense together. Now I want you to go in tomorrow and tell the coach you've changed your mind and you do want to play basketball. And tell your teacher you do want to take advanced calculus."

"I can't do that, dad."

"You can and you will. If you expect me to pay for your college, you'll be prepared for it the way I want you to be prepared."

"Now, dear . . ." George's mom started.

"Stay out of this, Mildred," George's father said angrily. "I can handle my own son. Damn psychologist."

"Dad, just listen," George said.

"I don't want to hear any more. You're going to talk to the coach and the math teacher and that's that."

"Dad, I can't do that. I've thought it through and I need to do what's best for me."

"What makes you think you know what's best for you?" his father challenged.

"Because I've had a chance to think about myself, what I'm like, what I want to work for."

"Well, that's what I'm talking about too. What you need to work for. And you need to be good in sports and good in math and . . . Why when I was your age, I not only played on the basketball team, I was on the swim team, I did cross country, and I took advanced calculus too. And I worked weekends in my uncle's store."

"Dad," George sighed. "I think that is terrific. I really mean it. I know you were something special and I'm proud of you for it."

"Well, then, why can't you be more like that?"

"That's the whole point, dad. That's you, that's not me."

"What do you mean, that's not you?"

"Dad, we are two different people. You were seventeen over twenty-five years ago. You lived as a high-school senior in that time. I'm seventeen today. I'm a different person. Times are different."

"What are you talking about? Times *are* different today. Of course I know they're different."

George continued, "The whole point is, this is a different time, a different person. And the person is me and I'm not you."

George's father stared at him.

George sat still, looking at his father, not daring to breathe. Would his father understand at all? He thought he saw a glimmer, a softening, a surprise, as if something had reached him, but then it disappeared.

"No son of mine is going to be a quitter."

At this his mom interrupted, "Dear, please. George is not a quitter."

George's father turned angrily to his mother. "You just heard him, didn't you? He's quitting. A good basketball player, chance to be a four-year *letterman* and he's quitting. A good mathematician and he's quitting."

George looked down at his plate. Sadness came over him. Where once he would have been hopping mad he was instead sad. He saw his father as someone fixed, resolute, unable to bend and change at all. He saw him as a person, very separate from himself, someone he had to live very close to but someone he really had a hard time relating to, a hard time even liking at times.

George's father started eating again. Then hurriedly he picked up his napkin, wiped his mouth, threw the napkin down and stalked out.

George's mother looked unhappily after him.

George finished his dinner making polite small talk with his mom about her fall flowers and whether or not they would have company for Thanksgiving as they usually did since Geraldine might come home.

George offered to help his mother with the dishes but she refused.

George avoided the living room where his father was sitting and went back to do his homework. He still felt unsettled and sad inside, yet he thought, "I've come a long way. Dad used to run me and push me and I was so mad all the time. I didn't think I could stand up to him because every time I used to try to stand up, I'd just get mad and get knocked down. This time I didn't think I could do it but I did. I was firm and reasonable and polite and it worked—it got me through without his winning. Of course, I didn't win either. I know he's going to be on me about basketball and calculus a lot the next few months. But I handled it this time, maybe I can handle it those times too."

George squared his shoulders. Today he felt more like a man than he had ever felt before. It felt good.

Some parent-child struggles are resolved fairly well, so that by the end of adolescence the young people relate more to their parents as adults and the parents respond to and accept their autonomy. In other cases, issues are not resolved and life-long conflict, of varying degrees can ensue. Parents find it particularly traumatic when a young person who has been following their guidance suddenly develops values, attitudes, or behaviors that are foreign to the parents. The parents then are thrust into the dilemma of providing guidance to a stranger who does not share many of their values and beliefs. The resultant conflicts are no one's particular fault and sometimes are not satisfactorily resolved.